BROOKE HOUSE TO BROOKE FIELDS

BROOKE HOUSE TO BROOKE FIELDS

Musings of an Engineer

Chandy John

PARTRIDGE

To order additional copies of this book, contact
Partridge India
000 800 10062 62
orders.india@partridgepublishing.com

www.partridgepublishing.com/india

In the beginning.

I started my studies in a Montessori School on Montieth Road, in Egmore, Madras for a year. The unfortunate part of this short story is that, this school does not exist today and in spite of my best efforts, I am unable to find out the full and original name of the Montessori School where I had studied. I then moved to Miss Bain's Church of Scotland Mission School in Kilpauk, Madras for Classes 2 to 5 and then moved from there to the original Madras Christian College High School in George Town, Broadway, Madras, for Form 1, in 1946 and then to the new School Building of Madras Christian College High School in Chetput, Madras from Form 2 to Form 6, passing out from this school in SSLC in 1952. Here the medium of instruction was in English, and Malayalam was my second language.

Though Madras Christian College High School had selected me for direct admission to the Intermediate course at the Madras Christian College in Tambaram, I chose to take admission in the Loyola College at Nungambakkam in Madras, because this college was not only well reputed, but only about 15 minutes by bicycle from home. Tambaram was more than an hour's journey to and from home, mainly by suburban electric train. I passed the Intermediate Group I examination in 1954. Here, at Loyola College, I took French as my second language.

Introduction to Mechanical Engineering.

About this time, my father bought an UK made AUSTIN A-40 DEVON Car, similar to the one shown below. I was so fascinated by the variety of technologies employed in the car that almost every Sunday, after lunch, when my father would take his usual afternoon snooze, I would shut myself in the garage, open different sections / parts of the car, to see how they were made and worked.

 For example, I would open the Carburetor, Starter, Generator, Distributor, Brakes, Turn Signal Indicator, Dashboard Instruments, Windscreen Wiper Motor Drive, etc., just to see what was inside and try to understand how they work. This continued for several months, without the knowledge of my father, until one day one of my sisters revealed this news to my father. Instead of shouting at, or abusing me for this mischief, my father took the whole incidents in a most unexpectedly positive manner. Considering that I had done all this, for so long, without causing any impairment or impediment to the Car, he insisted that I personally set right all future problems encountered in the car. From then, I did mostly all car repair jobs all by myself except de-carbonizing the engine and replacing the Clutch Discs, which I could not do without the physical help of an assistant being by my side.

I was greatly helped in these efforts by my cousin, George Mathew, a Mechanical Engineer, who loaned me his UK published Automobile Engineering Text Book, which was written mainly about and carried many photographs and drawings of the units employed in the then popular Austin A-40 Devon car and served as a very useful reference for my work with my father's car.

About the time I left school and started my Intermediate course in Loyola College, my long term ambition was to become a Doctor, but my exposure to my father's car completely turned my ambition around to engineering and automobile engineering in particular. With this ambition in mind, I started to engage myself in my studies very seriously, aiming to get into an engineering college, which my parents fully endorsed and supported. Accordingly I sought admission in and enrolled in Group I in the Loyola College, Madras.

In 1954, the then Madras State Government adopted a policy by which the number of students admitted to the College of Engineering, Guindy, Madras, from each district was to be proportional to the population of the respective districts. Accordingly, the total number of seats allotted to the district of Madras City, to which I belonged, was drastically reduced to four seats only, but I was fortunate to have been selected within this small quota of four.

I joined the College of Engineering (now called Anna University), Guindy, Madras, in 1954, for the B E Degree Course, taking Mechanical as the branch of my choice. Even though I was living in Egmore, Madras, I stayed in the hostel, as the journey to and from home would need more than a full hour each way, by suburban electric train and bus, with the College classes starting at 7:00 AM on all week days except Thursdays, when the classes started even earlier, at 6:30 AM, for Civil Survey classes.

However, my parents insisted that I leave the Hostel after the first year and attend college from home, based on their mistaken belief that my failure in the 1st year Mathematics exam was only because I did not study well, while staying in the hostel. This was the one and only time I ever failed in any school or college exam in my life. Mathematics has always been and still is the weakest link in my chain, right from school days, which I attribute mainly to my Mathematics teacher in MCCH School, who would openly shout and yell at any student if he made any mistakes. I did pass the Mathematics exam in my second attempt held during the middle of the second year.

My daily travel from home to the Engineering College was a tough exercise. I had to get up by 5:30 AM, get ready to leave for the college, walk almost a mile from home to the Chetput Electric Suburban Railway Station, then take the train from Chetput to Saidapet, walk about half a mile from the Saidapet

Railway Station to the Saidapet Bus Stand, take the 15 minute Bus ride to the Engineering College Main Gate and then the last 10 minute walk from the Main College Gate to the Class Room.

I was fortunate in that the Centenary of the founding of this college was held in 1956, when I was in the 3rd year. The preparations for and partaking in the Centenary celebrations was real fun for all of us.

It may be of interest to some to know that my engineering college is the second oldest continuously surviving technical educational institution in the world, the first such institution being a similar institution in Milan, Italy.

My engineering degree course required that every student do a formal apprenticeship during the vacation period of the 3rd year course, at a reputed and respected organisation. Considering that Sundaram Motors Ltd. a TVS Group Company, was a renowned and well-respected Automobile organisation and my special area of interest being automobiles, I applied for and got selected for apprenticeship at their main automobile workshop on Mount Road, Madras. It was indeed a very good exposure to several different well-known models and brands of automobiles, nearly all of which were imported around that time.

I was fortunate in yet another manner, whereby I was selected for a Government of India Scholarship to cover 50 hours of flying, free of cost. I secured a Private Pilot's 'A' License, after only 14 hours of flying experience in a De-Havilland

Tiger Moth single-engine, duplex-winged, two-seater aircraft, under a Tutor, whilst I was doing my third year engineering course. Though I enjoyed flying very much, I had no ambition to take up Flying as a career.

At the Engineering College, I would very often 'bunk' classes, making prior arrangements with anyone of my classmate friends to answer '*present*' when my roll call attendance number '*109*' was called out in the class-rooms.

I was very fond of western movies around this time and I remember how during one of my 4 years at Guindy, I saw exactly 100 movies in one calendar year. By the end of my 4 years of studies at this college, I estimate that I must have bunked about 60 % to 70 % of all classes put together. Yet, it is a wonder to me that I only narrowly missed securing a first class in my final year exam. This was because I took studies for my third and fourth year exams very seriously. Even though I was a day-scholar, I would very often stay back over-night in the hostel, sharing the single room of my very good friend R Narayana and gathering with a group, under a tree and with a lighted Electric Bulb hanging from the tree, for group studies, sitting up very late into many nights.

Start of my Working Career.

My work experience started in Madras in 1958, 2 weeks after I finished the very last exam of my final year and before the results of the exam were announced, as a Junior Engineer at the Central Workshops of the Madras Government Public Works Department. My main work comprised of designing and drawing of Sluice and Spillway Gates of Dams. During the six months I worked here, I was able to churn out independently quite a large number of drawings of different Sluice and Spillway Gates for a number of new Dams under construction within the then Madras State. This work involved adapting each Sluice and Spillway Gate to the specific requirement of each Dam, which varied from each other, in capacity, design, size, shape and style.

At this PWD Workshop, I reported directly to the Assistant Engineer, Late S Muthuvel, a college mate of mine, 3 years senior to me. He was exemplary, not only as a boss, but equally as a friend. He helped me so very well in learning all the tasks ahead of me that my working under him was more a pleasure than a burden. We shared interests in going fairly regularly to movies and an occasional dining out. He was instrumental in introducing me to western classical music.

To Melbourne, Australia.

During my final year at the Engineering College, I came to know that a college mate, one year junior to me, whose name I regret that I cannot remember now, had got through a Students' Exchange Program of the Melbourne University Student's Union, that facilitated a short 3 month visit to Melbourne for gaining practical work experience, during the long summer vacation between his third and final year courses. This news motivated both me and my long-time friend and class-mate Bekal Krishnamurthy to try for the same and both of us succeeded in getting accepted for the Exchange Program. Our plans involved going to Melbourne for one year and the two of us were quite happy to get this opportunity.

A few weeks before Kris and I were ready to depart for Melbourne, another class-mate of ours, D Raj (Rajagopala) Reddy, who is now at Carnegie Mellon University, Pittsburgh, USA, approached us and said that he would also like to come with us to Melbourne. So, we gave him all the required information and he applied for being selected. He was lucky to get his selection just in time to get all necessary Visas and Travel Tickets. Since all three of us thought it too expensive to fly all the way by air from Madras to Melbourne, we chose the most economical alternative means of traveling, namely, from Madras to Penang by ship, Penang to Singapore by train and from Singapore to Melbourne by air.

We landed at Melbourne and were allotted to stay at the University Students Hostel, Parkville, Melbourne, as most of the rooms at the Hostel were vacant at this point in time on account of Christmas vacation. As we had to vacate the Hostel at the end of the Christmas vacation, Krish, me and a third friend, Dr. Dinanath K Rangnekar (who got his PhD from the London School of Economics and joined the Melbourne University as the Head of the department of Asian Studies) decided to move together into a rented beautiful two bed-roomed fully furnished house, belonging to an ex-Czarina and her daughter from Russia, located at 33. Allambee Avenue, Camberwell, Melbourne. Raj Reddy chose to stay separately as a paying guest with an Australian / English couple.

Dr. Dinanath K Rangnekar, an Indian citizen, with a Kashmiri background was quite an intellectual giant and a social wizard. He had been invited by Melbourne University to start and head a new department of "Asian Studies" in the Melbourne University. Dinar, as all his friends affectionately called him, returned to India after one year at this University and joined The Economic Times as Editor and was personally responsible for a major transformation of this newspaper during its early stages. He then left The Economic Times and joined The Business Standard in Kolkata as Editor. He passed away at an early age, due to a heart attack, while he was working as Editor, The Business Standard, in Kolkata.

At The Australian Paper Manufacturers Ltd.

The stay of Krish and me in Melbourne involved working at three different places for four months each, all arranged by the Melbourne University Students Employment Board, with a view to get maximum exposure at different places of work. While both Krish and I strongly wished to work with an Automobile firm, there was no opening available at any of the Automobile companies in or around Melbourne, due to the severe ongoing depression in Australia at that time. So we accepted the first offer that came to us from The Australian Paper Manufacturers Ltd. who put the two of us through a rigorous and extensive work exposure program in all their various departments of their Paper Mills.

Raj Reddy, being a Civil Engineer, chose to work with the Country Roads Board (equivalent to the Highways Department) of the Government of Victoria.

At The Shell Company of Australia Ltd.

After the first allotted period of four months at APM, both Krish and I moved to The Shell Company of Australia Ltd. where work was going on at a very fast pace to set up the maximum possible number of Petrol Pumping Stations throughout the State, before the end of a deadline given by the Government. The two of us were assigned this work, along with a team of Australian and Italian Architects all reporting to the departmental head. An interesting observation during our time here was that the two of us from India, would churn out twice, or often more than twice the amount of work done by an average Australian or an Italian architect. This work involved making the detailed plan of the layout of complete Petrol dispensing Stations, within a given framework of rules which could be easily done for any plot that was nearly rectangular, or square in shape. However, one particular plot specifically assigned to me was of a triangular shape and not able to readily comply with all the given framework of rules of the Shell Company. Exercising my mind on this plot, I was able to plan out a very unconventional layout that was able to fully meet all the given rules, but the plan was so unconventional, that the head of the design and drawing department could not accept my plan in the normal course. Since there was no one in Shell Company, Australia to give a green signal to my radically unconventional plan, the departmental head therefore sent my proposed layout drawing to Shell, USA to seek their opinion, help and guidance for laying out the station on such an unconventionally dimensioned plot. To my biggest surprise, the reply came from Shell, USA showing a layout in a triangular plot, which for all practical purposes was almost identical to my layout. As my responsibility ended with completing this layout drawing, I never came to know whether this station was eventually built or not. Though our term at Shell Company was to have terminated in 3 months, the volume and pressure of work to meet the government's given deadline was so heavy that the Shell Company requested both of us to stay on for an extra period of one month, for which Shell sought and obtained approval from The Country Roads Board, Melbourne, our next employer.

At The Country Roads Board Workshops.

My tenure at the Country Roads Board Workshops at Syndal, Melbourne was the highlight of my stay in Australia, on account of several factors, the main factor being direct and immediate boss, Thurston Ashcroft, the Deputy Chief Engineer who spared no efforts to take a very keen and sincere interest to contribute his best efforts to train and develop our skills, knowledge, exposure and experience in every sphere of the different types of mechanical engineering work within his territory and command. I owe a lot of my present technical skills and knowledge to this one person, who has contributed a very big share in my technical growth and development. Thurston, who had worked earlier as Planning Engineer with Leyland Motors, UK, insisted that both Krish and I get familiar with personally driving of all varieties of heavy Earth Moving Vehicles like, Tractors, Earth Movers, single-engine and twin-engine Bull Dozers, Road Rollers, etc. He also arranged for both of us to travel to remote rural areas to observe and study their highly advanced Road Making Technologies, which could complete construction of totally new roads, at rates of up to about one mile a day. He also arranged for both of us to visit the factories of several other engineering companies in and around Melbourne, in order to enhance our exposure to different fields of mechanical engineering. Thurston was a gem and a giant of a person, who had a particular affinity towards all Indians and took a very special and deep personal interest and went all out of his way to make the stay of both Krish and me in Australia and with Country Roads Board in particular, truly beneficial in every possible way and spared no efforts to give both of us the widest possible variety of exposure and experience in as many fields of engineering as possible. Thurston's and his family comprising of wife and one daughter only, had a special leaning towards Indians which can be attributed to the fact that Thurston's father who spent many years in Russia, died in Lucknow, India and was buried there. While our term at CRB Workshops was to end after four months, or completing the total one year term, as originally proposed by the Melbourne University Students' Exchange Program, we were fortunate in that, thanks to Thurston's help both of us got an extension of Visa and continued with Country Roads Board Workshop for one more year.

Mrs. Treasure Southen.

Another person who played a major role in my personal growth and development was my hostess, Mrs. Treasure Southen, with whom my friend D Raj Reddy stayed as a paying guest for one year, until he moved from Melbourne to Sydney for his Master's Degree Course in Civil Engineering. When Raj vacated his room, another occupant of a second room at Mrs. Southen's apartment also happened to vacate the second room. Therefore, Mrs. Southen invited both Krish and I to come over as her paying guests and occupy the available two vacant rooms which we gladly accepted. Mrs. Southen, a graduate in Psychology from UK and a practicing Scientologist, was exceptionally hospitable and met all our needs in the most helpful manner. Mrs. Treasure Southen voluntarily accepted all Asians among our circle of friends under her tutelage, insisting that we all address her as "Mom". Though Mom never made any attempt to convert any one of us Asians, as Scientologists, I took some interest to read quite a few books on Scientology in her library, while I stayed with her, in order to satisfy my curiosity to know and understand what all the international controversies about Scientology from then, till today, were all about.

About this time, we got in touch with a fairly large group of Sri Lankan friends, prominent among who was, Siri Wijesinha, who is now in Colombo, Ramani Leanage, who is now in London and Malanee Wimalaratne, who is now in Melbourne. Siri was a perfect lady who took a mother-like interest and care of all Sri Lankan persons, both boys and girls, living in Melbourne. Ramani Leanage, was a chirpy and warm hearted girl, very fond of dancing. Malanee was going steady with Channa Wimalaratne, to make a perfectly lovable and friendly couple. Channa – a perfect gentleman, was more of an introvert, but socially warm towards one and all. Almost every weekend was a special occasion for us, when a sizeable number of Indians, Fiji Indians, Malaysian Indians, Sri Lankans and other Australian friends would get together at our residence in 33 Allambee Avenue, Camberwell, Melbourne, for dance and dinner parties very often.

Creativity.

Once when browsing through The Sydney Myer Mall (then the second largest Mall in the world, at that point in time) in Melbourne, I happened to notice a Paper Back Pocket Book with the title – "**Your Creative Power**", in the book shelf that caught my attention. I bought this book, read it and practiced several mental exercises mentioned in the book, which I believe has had a lasting and far reaching effect on me. This was when I was 23 years old and at a very impressionable and formative stage in my personal growth and development and there were many aspects covered by the book that impressed me very much, but I never gave much thought to this subject after reading the book and practicing the exercises, as my interests veered towards various other new and interesting subjects. Sometime in the mid-1970s, after I had joined Brooke Bond, I came across a news item in the TIME weekly newsmagazine which mentioned that Purdue University in USA was planning to start a Degree Course in the subject of "Creativity" and that they had explored the whole world for any books written on the subject of Creativity, to add the same to their University Library. The write up in the TIME magazine reported that Purdue University was dismayed to find after a very extensive search that in the whole world, there were only three books altogether written on the subject of Creativity, at that point in time and all the three books were written by one and the same author, "Alex Osborne". Remembering that I had purchased a book on Creativity, some years ago while I was in Melbourne, I went through my bookshelf in Kolkata and was surprised to find that the book I had purchased earlier was written by the same author "Alex Osborne". Today, I can assert and say that I cannot but attribute my present better than average creative abilities and talents to the same "Alex Osborne" and that his book has opened up a completely new way of life and a totally new world of opportunities for me.

At The National Tobacco Co. of India Ltd., Kolkata.

While in Australia, my elder sister, who was then in UK, wrote to me about a classified advertisement that appeared under the Code "YO64", inserted by The National Tobacco Co. of India Ltd. Kolkata, that appeared in the **Manchester Guardian**, inviting Indian Engineers with foreign work experience, for their works in India. Both Krish and I applied for the job and the company invited both of us for an interview at Madras by one of the company directors, as soon as we returned to Madras.

Both Krish and I were interviewed on the same day by the same Director, offered the same job, the same salary, holding the same designation – "Maintenance Engineer" at the same factory, both reporting to the same boss, S K Dey, Chief Engineer and shared the same office room in the factory in Kolkata. We also rented and shared a two bedded room in a Kolkata based hotel, for the first few weeks and later moved into a rented apartment at 27, Mahanirvan Road, near the Triangular Park, off Rash Behari Avenue, Kolkata.

A few weeks later Krish mentioned to an office colleague that he has no desire to continue in this job, which news on reaching the top, prompted the Director to call both of us together for a meeting, where we were asked the same question – "***What are your plans regarding continuing to work here?***". Krish frankly said that he is planning to go to UK for further studies, while I said that I am willing to continue to work here over a much longer period, but considering that I have no background or exposure to Tobacco related machinery, I can consider a long-term stay in the company only if I was granted training over a two year period at the various Tobacco Machinery manufacturer's factories in Europe. While Krish was requested to promptly submit his resignation, which he did, my request was accepted and necessary steps for my training at the various Tobacco related machinery manufacturer's factories in Europe was promptly taken up at the company's Head Office.

While I continued to work at this Cigarette factory, a few weeks later, the same Director asked me to check on the progress made about the various applications for my training abroad and the application to the government for my going abroad for this training. On looking deeper into the related papers, I was shocked and dismayed to find that the company had actually applied only for a total training period of 6 months, which the government had approved, as against my original request for a total of two years. I immediately made my own private plans to quit this job because I felt that this was not a company which honoured their commitment and so I should therefore look for an alternative job.

My futile attempt to return to Australia.

As entry into UK at that time was free and open to all Indians, I wrote to some 30 or 40 companies in UK seeking a job, but the universal reply I received from all companies and without a single exception, was that there was no scope for any job, because of the very heavy recession then in UK. So, I realised that the next best plan for me would be to go back to Australia, but this time for studies, supported by a part-time job to financially support myself and my newly married wife, Leela.

With this new plan in mind, I applied to Sydney University for a degree course in Production Engineering, which was accepted. In order to meet the requirements of the necessary Visa, myself and Leela first had to have a medical check and a medical fitness certificate, proof of accommodation, which I had secured at the YMCA for myself and at the YWCA for Leela. I also needed a certain minimum amount of Dollars in a Bank in my name. My ex-boss, Thurston Ashcroft was gracious to remit the required sum of money on my behalf and open the necessary new bank account in my name in Sydney. The last requirement was that I had to have a proof of being employed somewhere. Thurston had a good friend; James McDonald who ran a Road Roller manufacturing factory in Melbourne and at Thurston's request McDonald gave me an Appointment Letter as a Sales Engineer at his Sales Office in Sydney, as his only manufacturing operations was in Melbourne. There was an unwritten understanding that I would be paid the normal salary for a total period of four weeks only, within which time it was fairly easy for me to get a more suitable and satisfactory job elsewhere through the Sydney University Appointments Board.

Now, with all documents needed for applying for the Visas ready in hand, I resigned my job at National Tobacco Company, packed all our goods needed to be taken to Sydney, handed it to a Cargo Agent in Kolkata, booked the Air

Tickets for Leela and myself from Madras to Sydney and send the full set of required documents to the Australian High Commission at New Delhi for getting the Visa.

My brother-in-law, who then happened to be the head of the Audit and Accounts at Rashtrapati Bhavan (President's Estate) at New Delhi, checked with the Australian High Commissioner's Office at New Delhi and was informed that all our documents are fully in order and therefore the Visas can be expected to reach us in about two weeks, which would enable me to reach Sydney University before the University term starts on March 1st. Four weeks passed by with Leela and I waiting at Madras, with no Visas in hand and the Australian High Commission in New Delhi unable to give either me or my brother-in-law any reasons or explanations for the delay in granting the Visas. At my request, Sydney University had extended the last date for admission to end-March as a very special case, but it was of no help.

Around this time my friend Raj Reddy, who was then working as an Applications Engineer with IBM at Canberra, approached an official at the Indian Embassy in Canberra and they together visited the Immigration Department at Canberra (capital of Australia) to find out the reasons why the Visa was denied to us. They were informed that the Immigration Department had verified and confirmed, my admission at Sydney University, accommodation at YMCA for myself, at YWCA for Leela, enough money in my bank account, proper health certificates, but could not get any confirmation about my having been given the Sales Manager's job at McDonald's Sales Office at Sydney. Even though I was assured of a regular salary being paid for the first four weeks at Sydney, McDonald had not expected me to attend to, or do any work at his office in Sydney for these four weeks, as he was quite confident that I could easily land up with a more suitable job in Sydney within the first four weeks, through the Sydney University Appointments Board. Therefore, he had not thought it necessary that his Sydney Office should be kept informed about my appointment letter, which now clearly explained the full background to the Australian Immigration Department refusing the grant of our Visas.

When Thurston Ashcroft was informed about this background to our inability to get the Visas, he was so upset that he took up the matter seriously and directly with the Minister for Immigration at Canberra, explaining how my career had been very seriously upset due to a very trivial error in our Visa Application papers. The Minister apologised profusely and promised that our Visa for the next academic year would be assured and that all necessary arrangements would be made well in advance for the same, provided I confirmed immediately that I would make all necessary attempts to get the admission at Sydney University and satisfy all requirements for the Visas next year. As remaining idle with my parents at Madras for one full year was totally ruled out, I had no option but to decline the Minister's offer and start looking for a new job elsewhere.

Career with Brooke Bond India Ltd.

I applied to 3, or 4 companies in India for a job and Brooke Bond India Ltd., was the first company to which I had applied and also give me an offer, which I readily accepted.

My career in Brooke Bond India Ltd. started in the Kolkata Hide Road Factory in April 1963, where Ken Harrison, an UK expatriate and Factory Manager was my immediate boss. The first 3 months were devoted to getting familiar with all functions and operations of all the machines in operations at all departments in the factory and submitting weekly hand-written reports on all what I had learnt during the immediate past one week. My reports, along with similar reports of other trainees, were screened first by Ken Harrison, a well-qualified Mechanical Engineer, followed by E J Cox, Factories Director, then Frank Ward, Deputy Chairman and finally by J G Robinson, Chairman and Managing Director. I have every reason to believe that all my reports describing the workings of each type of machine and supported with very well-made hand drawn sketches of each type of machine in the factory would have left behind a very good impression in the minds of all those who went through my reports.

After my training, I was posted as a Manager in charge of the Gravure Printing and Paper Bag Making department. I had to take turns working on night shifts, for 5 nights a week, about once every month, in rotation with 3, or 4 other executives, taking full responsibilities for the running of the Tea Blending, Packing and the Gravure Printing and Bag Making departments in the night shift in the Kolkata factory and then revert to taking charge of the Gravure Printing and Bag Making department, during the day shifts of the next 4 or 5 weeks.

The quality of Pice Packet Paper Bags produced on all the 27 UK designed, but Brooke Bond India made Printing cum Paper Bag Making Machines at the

Bag & Printing Departments in the various Brooke Bond factories in India, were so bad that I was told by Ken Harrison that **'this Gravure Printing and Bag Making department at Kolkata is the central place for all Brooke Bond factories in India, where 'Bombs' are manufactured, distributed for explosion at the other Brooke Bond factories in India'.** He also informed me that virtually every mechanical engineer employed in Brooke Bond India Ltd., around that time had been assigned in the past, the task of debugging the various problems in these machines and every engineer, without a single exception, had completely failed in the task. Ken Harrison then added that I am now being posted here on a very long term basis and that I have to plan and implement all my future work, keeping this in mind.

An interesting daily routine during Ken Harrison's tenure at the Kolkata Factory was that he would go daily on an inspection walk round the whole factory, including the Bag and Printing Department where I worked. He would then make it a point to stop somewhere in the middle of the Bag & Printing Department factory floor and chat with me every day literally on any subject that he thought of, but rarely related to work. This chat would last for a minimum of half an hour and often go on for an hour or more, on a daily basis. Our conversations were usually very interesting and stimulating, as he was an intellectual person with very wide interests and knowledge.

Clement Wood's Tea Bulker/Blender.

One interesting episode at the Kolkata Factory was that the full set of the original Clement Wood's drawings of the "Tea Bulker", as the Silo/Tower type Tea Blending Machine was commonly called in those days, was kept very safely under lock and key inside a draw of Ken Harrison's writing table and was not accessible to anyone else, including the Head of Engineering Department, O

TOWER TYPE TEA BLENDING SYSTEM
with Tea Infeed Hopper flush with ground level
and provided with Magnetic Separator & Vibratory Sifter

P Kapoor. This was because the Bulker, or Blender was patented (Patent No. 20694 dated 14th March 1934) and no visitors were allowed to even enter the Bulking/Blending Department during those times, as the company had every intention of keeping all and any information about this Tea Bulker, or Blender a secret. I cannot be certain, but I suspect that I was perhaps the first and only executive in Brooke Bond to whom Ken Harrison had not only shown the original drawings but also explained in full detail the mysterious working principle of this truly unique machine. This Tea Blending machine along with a few other machines invented by Clement Wood played a very important role in the expansion and growth of Brooke Bond, not only in India (which had a total of seven Blenders), but also in Sri Lanka (which had two Blenders), Pakistan (which had one Blender), and in Kenya (which had one Blender).

In my opinion, it would be difficult not only for a lay-person, but also for an Engineer of more than average intelligence, to believe that even if he was allowed to enter into, look around and study the complete innards of the empty Blender, it would be quite difficult for him to really understand how the Blender went about making a good heterogeneous mix of quite a large quantity of Tea (normally 6 Tons of Dust grade Tea, or 4.5 Tons of Leaf grade Tea) without agitating, or stirring the Tea and only just controlling the fall of the Teas properly from the Upper to the Lower Chambers of the Blender, under gravity. I would even venture to say that even if the Engineer was allowed to see the actual fall of all the Teas from the Upper to the Lower Chambers, from inside the Blender, during its full operating cycle, he would not easily understand how the Blender went about making the very heterogeneous mix of quite a large quantity of Tea, without agitating, or stirring the Tea and causing damage of any kind whatsoever to the Teas. All this was achieved primarily by the simple manner and control of the fall of Teas, in a proper sequential manner, from the Upper to the Lower Chamber of the Blender under gravity. I would further venture to say that there is perhaps no Engineer who ever worked in Brooke Bond and alive today that can correctly and completely explain the full operating principle of how the Tea mixing is done by this Blender. In my opinion, the exact principle of operation of this Blender cannot easily be explained verbally, or in writing, or even with the help of conventional two-dimensional drawings. It can best be explained only by a properly designed and produced three-dimensional and animated color video movie, or a working see-through model. The full credit for this truly ingenious machine should go entirely to one gentleman, namely, Clement Wood, the then Factory Manager of the Kolkata Factory and Technical Director of Brooke Bond India Ltd. during the late 1920s and early 1930s. Clement Wood passed away in 1938.

Clement Wood's Pice Packet Packing System.

Clement Wood should also be given full credit for the creation of the Wood's Pice Packet Packing Machine and along with it, its complete Packing System (patented in UK in 1929), which from the very first day of its introduction, sometime in the 1930s, till today, that is a span of over 80+ years, can rightly claim to be **the cheapest automatic Retail Packing System for any product, in any size, using any Packing Material, in a Pouch or a Sachet form, anywhere in any country in the world.**

Clement Wood's Tea Processing (Cutting) Machine.

Clement Wood should also be given total credit for his creation of the Tea Processing (Cutting) Machines, patented by him in 1936, which for several decades helped to reduce the net cost of Tea used in certain blends by several million Rupees. While it can easily and wrongly be concluded that this Tea Processing Machine is just another Tea cutting, or Tea particle size reduction machine, I must assert that there is much more to it than just such a simple explanation. While the Wood's Tea Processing Machine can rightly claim its several unique features, its record of production output per hour, manpower requirement per ton of Tea and floor space requirement was beaten by the four German designed Eirich Mills, manufactured by John Fowler India Ltd., Bangalore and introduced by me, not only for the very first time in Brooke Bond India Ltd. but also used for processing (cutting) Tea anywhere. Two of these machines were installed at Kolkata, one at Coimbatore and one at Ghatkesar, all manufactured by John Fowler India Ltd., Bangalore. The net profit gained by employing the Wood's Tea Processing Machine, or the Eirich Mills during its lifetime would be truly staggering.

At Bag & Printing Department, Kolkata Factory.

Due to the very high humidity in Kolkata during a major part of the year, working even in the spacious hall of the new Bag & Printing Department at the Kolkata Factory was so difficult because even a few drops of perspiration falling from the hands or faces of the workers on the Paper Web under tension in the machine during operation would snap the web. This resulted in frequent interruptions to the running of the machine, loss of production and increase in waste of Paper and Ink, by way of spoils.

In order to help me in this matter, Dr. Roy Chowdhury, the then Kolkata factory doctor obtained a "**KATA Thermometer**", which is a special purpose temperature measuring instrument, consisting principally of an alcohol thermometer suspended in the middle of a closed Sphere that was coated on the outside with matte black paint. This special purpose Thermometer was used to measure the combined effect of radiant heat falling on the black sphere, air cooling power and, indirectly, the effect of small wind speeds in the air circulating around the black sphere and also by measuring the time taken for the temperature of the bulb of alcohol to make a specified drop (100° to 95°F), at any chosen spot in the hall. This Kata Thermometer was brought to India at the request of Dr. Roy Chowdhury, by a Brooke Bond expatriate coming from UK. Using this instrument and a ready reference chart, it was possible to get a meaningful number with which the degree of human comfort could be reliably measured and quantified. Using data obtained with the application of this Kata Thermometer it was possible to determine the specific and most uncomfortable locations in the hall and also understand what were the factors that were specifically contributing to discomfort at each of these locations and thereby help in determining what steps should be taken to minimise the discomfort at these locations.

With reliable data measured personally by Dr. Roy Chowdhury, over a period of about one year, a number of technically and financially viable and acceptable ideas and plans were progressively implemented, to make the discomfort level acceptable to work in this difficult environment. The alternate and obvious solution was to resort to unacceptably expensive total air conditioning of the department, together with a conventional False Ceiling below the Asbestos Sheet Roof, covering approximately 10,000 Sq. Ft. Amongst the other ideas and plans implemented by me were the scientifically designed and distributed three Spot Ventilation equipment and accessories, designed and supplied by the Swedish multinational, M/s Svenska Flaktfabriken (India) Ltd., Kolkata, the second of such an installation in India and a fleet of 30 Nos. of 18 inch diameter conventional Axial Flow Exhaust Fans distributed uniformly along the vertical roof truss line to exhaust the hot Air from the upper layers of the hall. Also, a fleet of UK designed, but India made special purpose Hot Air Exhaust Hoods, Ducts and Fans to not only expel the hot Air surrounding the 124 Nos. of 250 Watts Infra-Red Lamp Heaters employed to dry the Gravure Inks applied on the Paper by the 13 Gravure Printing and Paper Bag Making and Label Printing Machines running in this hall. This same arrangement also helped to maintain the inflammable and explosive Toluene and Xylene vapor levels inside the hall at a safer and more comfortable level and also to help speed up the Ink and solvent drying during the gravure printing operation.

After about 2 years I was assigned a very special/unusual position in the Kolkata Factory Organisation Chart, wherein I directly reported along one line, on administrative matters only, to A K Mitra, the then Kolkata Hide Road Factory Manager, but for all technical matters directly to A A Ferraby, the UK Expatriate Chief Executive - Technical, Brooke Bond India Ltd. I was to keep Ferraby, fully informed regularly with detailed reports of all my technical activities, every fortnight, over a period of more than one year, which I did.

My observations regarding Spur, Helical and Bevel Gears.

A very interesting technical development that took place around this time was my casual observation that the running Gears of the notoriously problematic Berkshire Bag Making and Gravure Printing Machines, when viewed directly under the light of any Fluorescent Tube Light, clearly gives a visible indication that the rotary motion of the Gears was not smooth and uniform. This gave me a very valuable and vital clue that there was something fundamentally wrong somewhere with the transmission of Rotary Motion, through the various Gears and or other rotating elements in these machines. Investigating this matter further, I found that there were several factors contributing to the erratic rotary motion of the Gears. The biggest single factor for this erratic behaviour was that all the Spur and Bevel Gears used on these machines were manufactured on Milling Machines, instead of on conventional / traditional Gear Hobbing Machines, or Bevel Gear Generating Machines. This contention of mine was proved right by seeing the dramatically improved consistency of quality seen in the Bags produced on this machine, by the use of one completely new set of Hobbed, or generated Spur and Bevel Gears, manufactured by Braithwaite & Co. Ltd., Kolkata, fitted to one machine. To follow up and assist me in this endeavor, an Electronic Variable Stroboscope, made by Philips India Ltd. was purchased and used to trouble shoot, diagnose and locate the precise source of each trouble in the mechanical drive of the machines and identify the major causes of the problems with all the Berkshire Gravure Printing and Bag Making Machines.

My steps to ensure parallelism and / or perpendicularity of Web supporting Shafts and Rollers.

Another very important observation I had made about this time was that the parallelism and / or perpendicularity of all Web supporting Shafts and Rollers to the true and imaginary main center line of the machine has a very vital role to play to ensure smooth, steady and uninterrupted course of the Paper Web through its very long passage over the 32 Web supporting Rollers distributed throughout the 6 Meters long and 2 Meters height of the machine. The effect of this anomaly is easily noticeable by the behavior of the Paper Web as it passed through the machine. Either the Web did not flow along a true straight path and/or the Web was tauter along one edge and quite slack along the opposite edge, resulting in the web following a zigzag path. The Gravure Printing and Paper Bag Making Machines were originally designed in UK in the 1950s by an engineer at Berkshire Printing Co., which was owned by Brooke Bond, UK, specifically for manufacture of the machines in India, without depending on expensive precision Boring / Plano-Milling Machines for the manufacture of its Main Support Frames, as is done traditionally for all such machines elsewhere. It was therefore necessary to find out a correspondingly cheap, simple and reliable method of measuring and ensuring near perfect parallelism between all Shafts / Rollers and perpendicularity of all Shafts / Rollers, against the true and imaginary center line of the machines. The only other known method that could be employed in such cases and was commercially available was to use an imported Optical Auto-Collimator, commonly used for very precise aligning very large, long and continuous Plants such as Ships, Aircraft, Paper Mills, or Electrical Power Generating Plants, etc. A full set of accessories together with an Optical Auto-Collimator being an extremely expensive Instrument, costing over Rs. 30,00,000/- per set, normally is hired or leased from companies dealing with such specialised work, on a contract basis, as buying the same for an occasional one-time application is unviable to most parties, anywhere. To the best of my knowledge, even today, companies possessing Optical Auto-Collimators that can be hired or leased from them, are extremely rare in India. Hindustan Aeronautics Ltd. is one of the very few organisations in India that I know of having and using such Optical Auto-Collimators in the manufacture of Aircraft.

My original, novel and comprehensive alternate solution which costs only a small fraction of one percent of the cost of an imported Optical Auto-Collimator is illustrated in the two pictures below. This ridiculously simple and cheap solution eventually did fully solve all the web-alignment problems of all the 27 existing Berkshire Printing Machines in India.

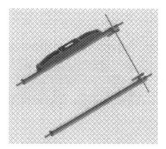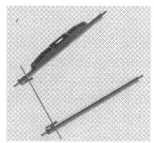

Introduction of Tolerances in Drawings.

The UK made drawings also lacked any mention of the required specifications regarding parallelism and / or perpendicularity of Shafts and Gear center-lines and regarding precision of center distances between adjacent gears within the required standard Tolerances.

Another observation I made was the lack of any manufacturing tolerances specified in the original UK made drawings of machine parts, making it difficult for the vendor / manufacturer to manufacture the parts exactly as required for the proper functioning of the parts in the machine. The original UK made Drawings did not specify any Manufacturing / Inspection / Assembly Tolerances for Parts wherever required, or applicable. I therefore got new Drawings made applying the currently and widely used Newall Tolerance System, which was the standard in vogue at that time. I had to get all these new drawings redone in less than the span of one year, when it became known that the Indian Statistical Institute had newly introduced ISI Tolerances, which was on the same lines as ISO Tolerances.

The UK drawings also lacked any mention of the required specifications regarding static and / or dynamic balancing, particularly for the rotating heavy parts, resulting in erratic rotary motion and consequent length variation of Pice Packet Bags, higher spoils and poor quality of Bags / Packets. The static balancing errors, particularly in the heavy Delivery Drums of the machines were rectified and this contributed to improving the uniformity of quality of Bags manufactured by the machines.

As sufficient manpower was not available in the factory to make the required large number of drawings, I was allowed to recruit three draughts men, especially for this work to be done directly under my supervision. As I had to go periodically on night shifts, about once every 4 to 5 weeks, these three draughts men would also come with me on night shifts in order to continue their work without interruption and directly under my supervision. The next set of problems to be dealt with was the lack of required set of Inspection Tools like Plug Gauges, GO / NO GO Gauges, Thread Gauges and Measuring Instruments, like Micrometer, Vernier, Depth Gauges, Height Gauges, etc., in the factory. All this was built up in reasonably short time and it became possible to inspect and accept only those vendor supplied parts that fully complied with all the specifications laid out in the new drawings.

Inspection of all parts supplied by Vendors was done till this point in time, by the Engineering department, where most technicians engaged in the inspection of dimensions and tolerances were not experienced in this type of task. For example, it was a standard joke amongst engineering managers in the factory that Vendor supplied Gears were inspected and rejected or approved by the Engineering Department Technicians only on the basis of counting the number of Teeth in the Gear conforming to the respective drawings or not. I therefore requested the Head of Engineering Department, O P Kapoor to arrange delivery of all new Vendor supplied and / or factory made parts, meant for use at all factories in India in their respective Gravure Printing and Bag Making Departments, to the Gravure Printing and Bag Making Department at the Kolkata Factory, where I worked. These parts were then inspected by technicians assigned for this task to work under my direct supervision. All good parts were accepted and any parts that failed to comply fully with all the specifications stipulated in the drawings were rejected, but only with my specific approval. This strict action on my part caused a lot of concern and agitation by the Vendors, but I stubbornly held my ground. Fortunately, the Head of the Engineering Department and the Factory Manager fully supported my position and the quality levels of machine parts progressively improved and reached near normalcy within about 24 months from the start of the initiation of the new inspection procedures.

Meeting with A A Ferraby.

Sometime after continuing with this arrangement and completing all my currently active major tasks required in the Calcutta Bag & Printing department and in the Engineering Department, A A Ferraby called me to his office and said that *'the company would like to promote you and send you to some other factory, but the company is really handicapped because the company does not have a suitable person to take over and finish the work started by you, at the Kolkata Bag & Printing department and also to implement the company's plans to execute similar work at all the other Bag & Printing Departments at the other factories in India. Therefore, the company has an idea to make use of your services to initiate an all India master plan of work, for which you have to prepare all necessary steps such that the complete work will be finished in about 6 months from now and then make yourself ready and available for your transfer'.*

Rebuilding of all Berkshire Gravure Printing cum Bag Making Machines.

This plan of work involved making the full set of new detailed and assembly drawings, assigning proper Part Numbers for the complete set of parts for the complete machine, preparing Spare Parts lists, Operating Manuals, ordering sufficient quantities of Spares, Bright Bars, Gears, Sintered Bushes, GO / NO GO and Plug Gauges, Thread Gauges, Vernier, Height and Depth Gauge, Precision Spirit Levels, Camel-Back Straight Edges, etc., assigning stock levels for the various spare parts to be held always in in stock, designing and getting made a number of new Jigs and Fixtures, and then planning the distribution of all these items, as required, to all the other factories from Calcutta.

I then set out to each factory, staying 4 to 6 weeks at each factory, in rotation, to explain the scope, objective and methodology of the work to be done and demonstrating / training engineers / technicians for the complete work of rebuilding one old badly manufactured machine into a re-built machine that was capable of delivering near perfect Pice Packet Bags, at each factory. This task was completed, on one machine at each of the 5 Moffussil factories, as required within the target date of 6 months, leaving each factory to implement the necessary work all by themselves, on their remaining machines.

This work involved closing most of the screw holes made on the Machine by filling the holes with metal plugs, riveting, filing and scraping the Machine Pads level, repositioning the Machine Frames flat and level and re-drilling and tapping new holes to a very much higher order of precision, with a view to ensure the goal of getting a near perfect straight run of the Paper Web right from the very beginning till the very end of the machine run, which was very essential for the smooth and trouble free operation of the machine.

Another part of the rebuilding work on these machines involved repositioning each and every component, or assembled unit of the machine, to ensure that each and every shaft, or shaft assembly of any web supporting unit were repositioned perpendicular to the imaginary center line of the machine and at the same time parallel to each other and all these new positions located permanently by providing new Dowel Pins to the respective Mounting Brackets, or Frames. Another part of the rebuilding work involved repositioning and realigning all Ball Bearing and Bush Bearing Housings of the machines supporting Shafts carrying Gears and these new positions permanently located within the specified dimensional tolerances by providing new Dowel Pins.

I am glad to say the this work was completed on all the remaining machines existing in all the Brooke Bond factories in India, in about 24 to 36 months, leaving behind the full fleet of 27 machines running all over India as totally trouble free in all its basic printing and bag making operations.

It would not be out of context to mention that while I was the head of the Gravure Printing and Bag Making department at the Kolkata factory, the bulk of the production of Pice Packet Bags were used in the Tea Packing Department of the same factory. I would therefore visit the Packing Department, time to time, to see how the Bags were behaving on the Packing Machines and also to discuss the various problems experienced by the workers in the Packing Department. This practice gave me a first-hand feedback regarding the quality of the Bags and the different needs for improvement of the Bags / Machines, instead of depending on a second hand feedback from a third person.

An interesting incident that happened while I was working at the Gravure Printing and Bag Making department was that a stranger walks into my office introduces himself as the owner of an engineering company and offers me a partnership in his company, if I would quit Brooke Bond and join him. Yet another incident that repeated twice was Ramesh Bhargava, Managing Director, Rollatainers Ltd., a company which had a very close relationship with Brooke Bond for well over half a century, requesting me to leave Brooke Bond and join Rollatainers Ltd. I could only politely decline these offers.

Major Modifications to the basic Wood's Pice Packet Packing Machines.

A very crucial and interesting development that resulted from my fairly frequent visits to the Packing Department was a major modification of the basic Pice Packet Packing Machine, resulting in the total elimination of two out of the four existing Main Packet Conveyor Belts above the Wood's Pice Packet Packing Machine Table Plate, which not only helped reduce the size of the floor space occupied by the machine by almost 50 %, but also simplify the total drive chain and gear mechanism and at the same time rid of many parts below the Machine Table, thereby helping to keep the floor space below the machines cleaner. This modification also indirectly helped improve the uniformity of top fold and the spacing between adjacent Pice Packets, thereby giving an aesthetically better display of the Pice Packet Strips hanging for display in Retail Shops.

Another interesting development during my tenure at the Kolkata Factory was that I partook in nearly all occasions of negotiations between the management and the two Trade Unions of the factory over the Periodic Long Term Agreements. I was the only departmental head of the whole factory included in the negotiating team from the management side because the management felt that I can play a very significant role in the negotiations with both existing Trade Unions, due to the very high degree of trust and confidence the workers of the factory and the two Trade Unions had in me as a person.

An indirectly related incident took place after I was transferred from Kolkata to Coimbatore Factory, when a Management and All India Trade Union negotiation was being held in Bangalore at The West End Hotel. As I was visiting Bangalore from Coimbatore during this time, in connection with some other work, I was instructed to take a sealed envelope from Coimbatore and hand it over personally into the hands of H D Moses, the Administrative

Officer of Coimbatore factory, the contents of which I had no knowledge. When I reached the West End Hotel, the negotiations had just taken a break and the whole negotiating group was outside the meeting hall, having a Coffee break. Seeing me, the group of the Kolkata Factory Workers surrounded me to have a chat with me. They insisted that I meet their Communist Party official representative, whom I had never met before, other than seeing him from a distance, addressing the factory workers at the periodic factory gate meetings. This Party leader came forward, shook hands with me and remarked that he has heard lots of good stories about me, but never had the opportunity, or privilege of meeting me. He then added that the Calcutta Factory workers are very disappointed about my transfer from Calcutta to Coimbatore and considering that it is inappropriate for the Trade Union to formally make the request, he wanted me to appeal to the management to get me transferred back to Calcutta. My obvious response to this request was that I cannot make such a request and the matter ended there.

I must also mention here that my relationship with all the Trade Union leaders both at the Kolkata Factory and at the Coimbatore Factory were near perfect. While the workers and the Unions of Coimbatore factory acknowledged the big role I played in improving the machines and the factory environment, they wanted me to take up an equally big role in improving the working and service conditions of the staff and workers in the factory.

I Balasundaram, Technical Director.

A noteworthy period of my tenure in Brooke Bond India Ltd. was when I Balasundaram was my immediate boss and the Technical Director. He was a very admirable person, very well balanced in his relationship with all subordinates working under him and at the same time, quite strong in technical knowledge. He encouraged and supported everyone who worked under him with an even hand. During my tenure in Coimbatore factory, where I implemented several technical innovations, Balu, as many colleagues affectionately called I Balasundaram, as my boss never denied me any opportunity to undertake any plan of action and always gave his approval to any request I made for sanction of money required to execute the plans I had in mind. I am truly glad to say that on my part, I never let him down in any instance for which he supported me.

Dr. C A Varghese, Technical Director.

When Balu resigned from Brooke Bond, Dr. C A Varghese took over as my immediate boss and Technical Director. Though he served in this position only for a few years, he supported me in every possible way and in particular in initiating me to undertake the plan for upgrading and modernizing the Pice Packet Packing System, which was the topic that commanded my maximum attention over my 20 years' career span in Brooke Bond till that time.

M M Bhattacharjee, Technical Director.

When Dr. C A Varghese resigned from Brooke Bond, M M Bhattacharjee took over as my immediate boss for a short period.

John R Bee, Technical Director.

M M Bhattacharjee was followed by John R Bee, an UK Expatriate as Technical Chief Executive and my immediate boss for a short period.

Siebler Sachet Packing System employed together with my innovations.

The Siebler Sachet Packing System when employed together with my innovations, even though was overwhelmingly superior to the Wood's Pice Packet Packing System in every way and without even a single exception, would have been an even more attractive a proposition in today's modern Indian markets to compete even against any competitor's latest Sachet Packing System, imported or otherwise, not only for packing Tea, but for any other powdery, granular and free-flowing product.

To mention only the major benefits of the Siebler project, they are as follows: -

- Major contribution to Tea factory modernisation, production and space saving,
- Possibility of subsequent mechanization of secondary packing,
- Elimination of leaky packets,
- More rigid packets, better able to retain its shape during transport and handling,
- Packet offering full, uninterrupted printing surface on both sides,
- Packet difficult and expensive to duplicate, compared with existing presentation, which can be imitated relatively easily,
- Flexibility of new system for other sachet and strip presentations,
- Exploitation of Company's under-utilised machine building facility,
- Possibility of third party sale of machines for packing a range of products.

The importance of Pice Packets compared to the total Tea activity by the company can be seen listed below: -

	1985/86 (Actual)	1986/87 (Actual)	1987/88 (Budget)
% of BBI Packet Tea Tonnage	14.9	15.1	14.3
% of BBI Packet Tea Sales Value	15.9	14.9	14.8
% of BBI Packet Tea T. O. C.	24.5	18.0	18.4

Clement Wood's Tower type Tea Blender.

Amongst Clement Wood's many other notable contributions is, the unique Tower type Blender patented in 1934 and used to blend Tea. It was truly exceptional in that in my opinion it was and still is:-

1. The best Tea Blender in the world that can offer the highest output of blended Tea per hour, per Ton of installed capacity per hour.
2. The best Tea Blender in the world that requires the lowest man-power, per Ton of installed capacity per hour.
3. The best Tea Blender in the world that requires the least total HP of Motor Power, per Ton of installed capacity per hour.
4. The best Tea Blender in the world that requires the least electrical energy, per Ton of installed capacity per hour.
5. The best Tea Blender in the world that occupies the least floor space, per Ton of installed capacity per hour.
6. The best Tea Blender in the world that requires the least capital investment, per Ton of installed capacity per hour.

Clement Wood's unique Rotopan.

Another notable contribution of Clement Wood was the Rotopan, with which it was possible to have fully automatic, continuous and fast dispensation of a fairly accurate weighed quantity of Tea varying from about 25 to 250 Grams, or more, without the use of any Battery, Electric Power or Electric Motors, for application in Hand Packing Benches, at remote locations and / or where electric power was not available. As the Rotopans have all been scrapped by now (as they did not comply with the Weights and Measures Act introduced in 1976), I personally would have loved to see some working models of these Rotopans made and carefully preserved to show future generations, this truly unique product, which probably came into being even much before the popular UK designed and made Southall & Smith, or Southall & Driver electrically operated automatic Weighing and Dispensing Machines first appeared in the market.

Clement Wood's Tea Processing (Cutting) Machine.

Another notable contribution of Clement Wood was his 'Tea Processing (Cutting) Machine', patented in 1934 and revised in 1936, which could cut Tea Particles of any size, to any smaller sizes without generating excessive fine Tea Dust, or result in any significant loss of Bloom (called Greying by some in the Tea trade). This machine can be considered as equivalent to the original SAVAGE Tea Cutter used for an identical purpose. However, in my opinion, the Wood's Tea Processing Machine unlike the Savage Tea Cutter offered a very much higher output per hour and was infinitely and easily adjustable to cut Tea Particles to any desired size within its upper and lower limits, with minimum deleterious effects to the particles of Tea. All the Wood's Tea Processing Machines were scrapped and disposed of, after I introduced the German designed and John Fowler India Ltd. Bangalore made Eirich Mills which gave a much higher output per hour, with very much less requirement of manpower and occupying much less floor space, to replace all the existing Wood's Cutting machines operating in India.

When I joined Brooke Bond India Ltd. in 1963, a KORA Pice Packet containing 3 Grams of Tea was sold in the retail market for 3 Paise (Rs. 0.03). All the Wood's Pice Packet Packing Machines were running at 90 Packets per Minute at that time. At my suggestion and with my initiative, in technical terms, over some years, this speed was progressively increased starting from sometime in 1966/67 from 90 to 100, then to 120, then to 150, then to 200 and finally to 220 Packets per Minute, by about 1975, all over India. As the worker's incentive earnings were based on the actual total production achieved, some workers would put on Adhesive Tapes onto the Machine Drive Pulley to increase its diameter and thus un-officially increase the speeds of their machines further up to 240, in order to earn more incentive wages. Even though it was possible for me to increase the speed to 240, or even well beyond that, I did not do it, as I knew that it was not possible for the vast majority of workers engaged on these machines to continuously and manually collect and collate the finished Packets over the whole day comfortably, working continuously at speeds beyond 220, while only a few could do so at a speed of 240. Thus, the Wood's Pice Packet Packing Machine had reached its peak workable and universally acceptable working speed limit of 220 Packets per Minute, by about 1970s and the daily sales of all sizes of Pice Packets put together was approximately 10 million.

After Dr. C A Varghese took over from I Balasundaram as Technical Director and about the same time, it was initially proposed that I be moved from Coimbatore as Factory Manager of the Centron Blade Factory in Aurangabad and accordingly, I went to Aurangabad for 2 weeks, with a view to select and arrange for a place of stay for myself and my family. Though a flat was selected, there was a change in the line of thinking at Brooke House, Kolkata as I was asked to move to Calcutta as Engineering Manager.

After moving to Calcutta, Dr. Varghese mentioned to me that – *'the existing Pice Packet Packing System has reached its maximum possible operational levels in terms of Speed, Productivity, Machine Performance, Packing Material Consumption, Spoilage, Visual Appeal, Total Manufacturing Cost, Total Quality and has very limited scope to be improved any further and you being the main architect for virtually all these past improvements, I now want you to take up improvements to the next higher level. For this, you can go anywhere in the world, for as long as you require'*. It has to be mentioned here that I had not conveyed or indicated in any manner to Dr. Varghese, or to anyone else in Brooke Bond India Ltd. or anywhere else, at any time, that I had, or was even aware of a functionally and economically better and workable solution to improve the Pice Packet Packing System any further. At that point in time, I myself was not even aware of any better and cheaper alternate workable solution in any form anywhere.

It would not be out of place to mention here that, when Frank Ward, the then Deputy Chairman solicited suggestions from all executives, in September 1966, to improve any of the existing Packing Systems, I had then put forward one suggestion, in a two-page hand written note, supported by a mock specimen Pice Packet, (I still retain with me, for sentimental reasons, a carbon copy of my original hand written proposal and a mock specimen of the proposed Pice

Packet,) to replace the existing style of forming, filling and sealing the Pice Packets. A typed copy of my original hand written note is shown below.

PROPOSAL FOR A MODIFIED PICE PACKET

It is proposed to Form, Fill and Seal Tea Pice Packets all in one machine from pre-printed Paper Reels.

The method of operation for the production of the proposed packets is as follows: -

1. Paper Reels would be printed and re-reeled on one machine. This can be done by utilizing the print-end of the Berkshire Printing Machine and attaching to it a Re-reeling Device. In this operation, the only functional limit is the drying of Ink, which on existing machines is 250 feet per minute. With appropriate improvements to the machine and its drying arrangements, speeds up to and over 1,000 feet per minute can be achieved.

2. Packet forming and making would be done in a continuous in-line process from the pre-printed reel. The process of Packet Making would be done in the following continuous sequence – Gumming, Folding, Filling, Forming, Perforating, Slitting the required number of Packets per Strip and Collating. A device is to be provided to synchronize and if necessary alter the position of the printed panel with respect to the finished Packet. This principle of operation offers the scope to operate the machine at higher speeds.

The advantages of this proposed Tea Pice Packet are as follows: -

1. A saving of about 33 % of the total quantity of Paper over the existing type of Packet, while offering a finished Packet of the same size.

2. A better appearance to the finished Packet with no folded Flaps with both sides identical for display. The full area of both sides can be utilised to print the required panels.

---

3. The Packets can be made in the form of a continuous Strip of any convenient number, say 10 or 12, with Perforations to tear-off each individual Packet from the Strip. A hole can be punched in each Packet on one of the top corners to facilitate suspending the Strip from a Nail, or a Hook. Alternately, the required number of Packets can be attached individually to a String at the required distance.

4. The spoilage on both Printing and Packaging Machines would be considerably reduced as the proposed Tea Pice Packet needs only one single folding, against the existing side seam folding, top and bottom end flap folding.

Submitted by: -
CHANDY JOHN
Hide Road Factory
September 1966

The photocopy of the old specimen of the mock up Sachet is shown here. The feedback I got later from Head Office regarding my suggestion was that my suggestion was too farfetched and therefore beyond the scope of any implementation in the near future. I have not followed up on this nor given even one small thought over this suggestion afterwards, primarily because I by myself could not contribute anything, at that point in time, to make this suggestion a reality.

Little did I know then that less than 20 years later, I would personally and almost single handed, develop such a Packing System that was even much more technically advanced.

Over the next 6 to 9 months, after Dr. C A Varghese's talk with me, I subscribed to several reputed international magazines on the subject of Packaging and

Printing and also made extensive studies and inquiries with different companies in different countries all over the world, about any similar or equivalent Sachet or Pouch Packets, Sachet or Pouch Packaging Machines and Packing Systems in use anywhere. I then worked out a master plan only to explore possibilities to make up a totally new Pice Packet Packing System, by visiting a total of 35 different major Packaging Machine and Printing Machine manufacturers in 6 different countries of Europe, in one single trip, spread over a total span of 35 days. This plan was approved by the company and then followed up by me. The list of 35 factories of companies and countries visited by me in Europe, during this single trip, can be seen down below in **Annexure B**.

After my return, I prepared a Project Report presenting my findings, plans and proposals, which implied implementing a totally new and original Sachet Packing System, for the first time anywhere in the world, at that point in time and possibly even today. This totally new Sachet Packing System not only offered a far superior marketing and aesthetic appeal, compared to the existing Brooke Bond Lipton India Ltd.'s Wood's Pice Packet Pouch Packing System, but also required far less manpower, less total cost of Packing Materials involved and implemented at a very small fraction of the total capital cost compared to what it would have cost if implemented anywhere, in any advanced countries of the west.

This total project cost budgeted at about Rs. 4,75,00,000/- , if fully executed would have reduced the direct manpower involved in Pice Packet production by over 53 % (330 men, or some 11 % of the then total manpower engaged only in the factories concerned and as at the time of preparing the Project Report) costing Rs. 10,700,000/- p.a. The same Project, as at the time of preparing the Project Report, showed an Internal Rate of Return of 21.0 % and an Undiscounted Pay-Back Period of 6 years 10 months, which was extended only because of the consequence of an initial development period of 2 years before machine introductions into the factories speed up.

Here, I must express my sincere, heartfelt appreciation and gratitude to Dr. Varghese for having reposed such complete trust and confidence in me by entrusting this totally new and raw project to me, which was executed single handed by me and without anyone else anywhere checking or even overseeing my plan of action, or work, or supporting me and that too without any suggestion, evidence, claim, or proof of a successful outcome of a viable solution from me. I am glad to say that in the end, I did not fail to come up to Dr. Varghese's expectations.

One day, C S Samuel, the then Chairman and Managing Director asked me, "*What has happened to your Project Report?*" I replied that '*the report is fully ready, but it was too late to be included in the current year's Capital Expenditure Proposals, which has already gone to Unilever PLC, London for verification, clearance and approval and therefore my Project Proposal can only be included in the next year's list of Capital Expenditure Proposals*'. To this he responded – "*You give me the Project Report and I will see to it that it is included and approved along with this year's Capital Expenditure Proposals*". I am glad to say the Project Report was forwarded by C S Samuel, returned with approval and sanction to go ahead with the first Stage of the Project by Unilever PLC, UK, within a few weeks' time.

Auke Van de Clerk's visit to Bangalore.

Prior to the approval and sanction of the Project by Unilever PLC, UK, Auke Van de Clerk, Chief Engineer, Unilever PLC, UK was assigned to come to Bangalore, meet me and my new and immediate superior at that time, UK expatriate, John R Bee, along with his predecessor, M M Bhattacharjee (during whose tenure I had prepared the major part of this Siebler project report) to discuss the project details, before being granted clearance from Unilever PLC, London. Before, during, or after the meeting Van de Clerk, a very experienced and knowledgeable engineer, could not find even a small flaw in my report, nor contribute any suggestion, or idea to improve upon the whole project. At the end of the meeting, held at Taj Residency (now named as Vivanta) Hotel, Bangalore, Van de Clerk openly mentioned to me, that – '*for this one Project Report alone, Chandy, you really deserve a PhD*'. John R Bee and M M Bhattacharjee are witnesses to this remark, made in their presence by Van de Clerk.

It is necessary and important to mention here that no other individual, or group anywhere in Brooke Bond Lipton India Ltd. or in Unilever, London or in Rotterdam, or anywhere else, at any time were involved in investigating, working on any plan, idea, analyzing, preparing, suggesting, contributing or modifying this Project Report, other than Alan Fernandez, General Manager - Finance, whose only role was to vet and re-present the financial calculations involved in the Project Report and my immediate boss, John R Bee who helped to polish the language used by me in my draft of the Project Report. I would also like to emphasize here that the fact that no contributions were made by anyone else, was not because I kept all information close to my chest, or did not want to disclose anything of my line of thinking, ideas, or plans to anyone, but only because there was no one in Brooke Bond Lipton India Ltd. at that time with whom I could have had a healthy, constructive and intelligent dialogue on this subject.

All the required steps to be taken to implement this project were taken up in time and orders placed to manufacture and procure the required machinery, equipment and accessories required for the first phase of the project from various parties both in India and abroad. The first phase of the project comprised of the import of only one complete and standard Siebler Packing Machine and purchase of one full set of Siebler Packing Machine Manufacturing Drawings from Siebler Verpackungstechnik GmbH + Co. KG., (the erstwhile family owned company, by now taken over by the Piepenbrock Group, the largest Window Cleaning Group in Europe). It was further planned to manufacture all remaining requirement of 26 Packing Machines at the Brooke Bond's Development & Machine Building Factory at Kolkata, based on drawings obtained from Siebler and import five Hot Melt Adhesive Heating and Pumping modules from Nordson, USA and five Hot Melt Adhesive Pattern Coating and Application modules from Nordson, Japan.

Invention of the Collator to work with the Siebler Sachet Packing Machine.

Siebler had made it abundantly clear, right from the very beginning, that they will supply only their basic and standard Sachet Packing Machine, adapted to our size of Pice Packets and nothing more than that. Therefore, a special Collator was invented, designed by me and made at Brooke Bond India's Development & Machine Building Factory at Kolkata, to attach the same with Siebler's Pice Packet Packing Machine working at up to 1,000 Packets per Minute, in order to automatically produce and deliver separately and in-line, each finished bundle of dozen Packets, in the desired pleated and orderly manner. This Collator was made, tested and proved to run satisfactorily at the Development & Machine Building Factory in Kolkata and then sent to Siebler in Germany for being attached to the Packing Machine, tested, fine-tuned and then to be exported back to India together with the Packing Machine.

Pattern Coating of Hot Melt Adhesive.

The project also involved import of five custom-made Hot Melt Adhesive Application Modules made by Nordson, Japan, (Nordson Group being the world No. 1 in this field) to suit and work with the five simple and cheap Brooke Bond Lipton India Ltd.'s UK designed, but Indian made 4-colour Gravure Reel Printing and Rewinding Machine, to produce the special and unique Packing Material, required for use with the Siebler Packing Machine. Nordson, America was to supply five standard Hot Melt Adhesive Storage cum Heating cum Pumping Modules, to supply the molten Hot Melt Adhesive to the Nordson Japan's Hot Melt Adhesive Application Modules. It is worth mentioning here that any equivalent Printing cum Hot Melt Adhesive Pattern Coating Machine combination, that can produce the Packing Material as required for the Siebler Packing Machine Project, if imported from any European country, UK, USA, Japan, etc., would have cost a minimum of ten times as much or even more, as at the time of preparing the Project Report and even much more today.

Nordson, Japan was to supply a Hot Melt Adhesive Coating Application Module, of a profile similar to the profile of the existing Gravure Printing Modules of the Berkshire Printing cum Rewinding Modules of the machine made at Development & Machine Building Factory, Kolkata, in order to facilitate compatibility with the designs and drives of the other Gravure Printing and Rewinding Units of the machine and with minimum need for any changes to the basic design of the Printing Machine Main Drive Frame. A complete set of Base Plate, Side Frames and Impression Roller mounting components were made at Development & Machine Building Factory, Kolkata and sent to Nordson, Japan, with a view to help reduce the total cost of the complete Module to be supplied by them.

Printing cum Hot Melt Adhesive Pattern Coating Machine

A picture of the prototype 3 colour Gravure Printing cum Hot Melt Adhesive Pattern Coating Machine partially manufactured and fully assembled at the Machine Building Factory in Kolkata can be seen below: -

Hot Melt Adhesive, imported from National Adhesives and Resins Ltd., UK.

Sufficient Hot Melt Adhesive was imported from National Adhesives and Resins Ltd., UK, the world's largest Adhesive manufacturing company and a company within the Unilever Group. The required particular grade of Hot Melt Adhesive was selected after several meetings I had with Basil Ford, Export Manager, National Adhesives and Resins Ltd., UK, who would make routine monthly visits to India to market their products. Four Paper Rolls of Packing Material as required by the Siebler Pice Packet Packing Machine were produced in Kolkata with the required printed matter on one side and the unique Hot Melt Adhesive Registered Pattern Coating on the opposite side and sent in Roll Form to Siebler in Germany for testing and trials, before sending the finished Packing Machine to us in India.

My proposal to visit Siebler, Germany.

I proposed to K K Nair that I be permitted to visit Siebler in Germany in order to check that the prototype machine's performance was satisfactory and acceptable in all respects, before Siebler exports this machine to us in India. This suggestion of mine was not accepted, as I was told that a cheaper solution was possible by getting Auke Van de Clerk, Chief Engineer, Unilever PLC., UK, to go from UK to Siebler's factory in Germany, test and certify the satisfactory working of the machine, before being dispatched to India.

Report of Van de Clerk's visit to Siebler, Germany.

Van de Clerk after his visit to Siebler reported that the machine does not satisfy three conditions stipulated in the Purchase Order, namely that,

1. The machine cannot run at a speed of more than 800 packets per minute (or 80 cycles per minute in ten rows), as against the required speed of 1,000 packets per minute (or 100 cycles per minute in ten rows), mentioned in Siebel's Technical Brochure, specified in our Purchase Order and accepted by Siebler. This deficiency was reported as only on account of the low density and consequent slow fall of the very light Tea as the Tea fell from the Packing Machine's Volumetric Dozer into the Sachet, as it was being formed in the machine (while the same machine could deliver the expected 1,000 packets per minute with Sugar, as Sugar was heavier / denser). Siebler had no solution to offer to overcome this limitation with Tea. This fact was not reported to me earlier by Siebler and I came to know about it only from Van de Clerk, after his visit to Siebler's factory.

2. The machine does not seal the four edges of the Paper joints of the Sachet coated with 8 GSM Hot Melt Adhesive, as prescribed by Siebler. Siebler maintained that this problem was only on account of the use of a wrong Hot Melt Adhesive (recommended, manufactured and supplied to us from UK by National Adhesives and Resins Ltd. the world's largest Adhesive manufacturing group and also a Unilever company). Siebler subsequently proved their claim by demonstrating fully satisfactory sealing of the Paper joints of the Sachet with the same 8 GSM coating of a different Hot Melt Adhesive they had obtained from a German Company, namely, H B Fuller. This demonstration was done by a Siebler engineer in Calcutta, in the presence of M M Bhattacharjee, A K Sengupta and me, after the machine landed in

Calcutta. The fact regarding failure of the sealing of the Hot Melt Adhesive pattern coated Paper sent to Siebler for trials was not reported to me by Siebler and I came to know about it only from Van de Clerk, after his visit to Siebler's factory. Even though Siebler convincingly proved that the 8 GSM Hot Melt Adhesive Coating does work satisfactorily, K K Nair would not accept this proof, contending that the Hot Melt Adhesive Coating of the coated Paper used by the Siebler engineer was not pattern coated as it would be in the actual production run. K K Nair, apparently did not accept that pattern coating of the Hot Melt Adhesive was not the factor under test, but the feasibility of sealing with a 8 GSM Hot Melt Adhesive Coating.

3. The Collator made and tested in the Development & Machine Building factory in Kolkata and found to work quite satisfactorily during simulated trials carried out in Kolkata, before being dispatched to Siebler, could not be attached to and made to fit and work with the Packing Machine, in the required correct location by Siebler. This was on account of an obstruction caused by one of the four Support Legs of the Packing Machine. In my opinion, this limitation could very easily have been overcome, by either suitably modifying this Support Leg, or shifting the position of this Leg. I would have suggested and persuaded Siebler to accept this solution, if I was either informed by Siebler of this handicap, or if I was assigned the task of going to Siebler's factory, instead of, or with Van de Clerk. It is also to be noted that at no point in time did Siebler mention that there was any problem, anywhere, on this account, until we heard from Van de Clerk, after his visit to Siebler's factory.

Van de Clerk reported that Siebler had very strongly expressed to him their unwillingness to retain the machine with them any longer, for any further work in Germany, as the machine was complete and lying idle with them for the past several months, without having received any advance payment whatsoever on this account, as the Purchase Order was placed and the Letter of Credit opened without giving any Advance Payment to Siebler. However, Siebler had assured that they would extend their full technical support and co-operation to us, to solve any of the remaining problems, after the machine was delivered to us in India.

Auke Van de Clerk's recommendations.

Van de Clerk recommended that we accept Siebler's offer and not to take a line of confrontation with Siebler. Van de Clerk also repeated this recommendation to me privately, during one of his subsequent visits to Brookefields in Bangalore, but I had to promptly and politely break my dialogue with Van de Clerk in this matter, as I felt that it was not proper on my part to tell him that – *'I fully agree with you Auke, but I regret to say that it is only my boss, K K Nair who is opposing this position and he is unwilling to change his stand'*.

Siebler's faults.

I would specifically fault Siebler for not reporting immediately back to me when they found that the machine will not work at the expected maximum speed of 100 cycles per minute. It is not that neither I nor Siebler could do anything about it, but it was important that we were forewarned about this shortfall.

I would specifically fault Siebler also for not reporting immediately back to me, when they found that the Hot Melt Adhesive coated Paper Rolls send from India was not working as expected, so that I could have taken up the matter with National Adhesive and Resins Ltd. to arrange supply, on a priority basis, the required alternate / improved / correct Adhesive, to carry out further trials.

Alternately, Siebler could have even suggested that we contact H B Fuller, Germany, for the supply of the right grade of Hot Melt Adhesive for a very satisfactory solution, as we were not made aware of this alternative solution and we were not under any obligation, or under any pressure from anywhere to buy the Hot Melt Adhesive only from National Adhesives and Resins Ltd., UK, even though it was a Unilever company.

I would likewise specifically fault Siebler also for not reporting immediately back to me when they found that the Collator could not fit the Packing Machine, so that I could have worked on finding a workable solution, which was not very difficult. Neither did Siebler take any initiative to resolve this simple problem by themselves at their end.

Siebler's dispatch of the Sachet Packing Machine.

Soon after, Van de Clerk's visit and return to UK, Siebler sent a Telex message informing that they are ready to dispatch the machine to India and I promptly replied by Telex that the machine should not be dispatched, as it does not satisfy all the requirements stipulated in the Purchase Order. In spite of my telex and without responding anything to my telex message, Siebler did dispatch the machine to Kolkata along with the Collator, contrary to the instructions given in my telex message and by default collected the full due payment as stipulated in the Purchase Order and Letter of Credit.

K K Nair's reactions and decision.

K K Nair was absolutely furious with Siebler on hearing this and instructed the Company Secretary, Shyamal Sen to immediately take all necessary steps to file a case in the Kolkata courts against Siebler in order to get the Court's Order to return the machine to them and collect refund of all monies paid to them. This plan was very strongly opposed not only by Shyamal Sen, but also by the Kolkata based eminent and senior external lawyer, Sudipto Sarkar, who was assigned to handle this case, on the grounds that even if by some remote and unlikely chance we do win the case in India, the judgment cannot be enforced on Siebler in Germany, as an Indian court's judgment has no jurisdiction in Germany. To file and fight a fresh case in Germany to recover the money collected by Siebler was not even considered as an option. This only shows the abject and miserable lack of basic / fundamental knowledge of the legal processes (leaving aside the abdominal ignorance of the technical matters) involved in this Siebler Pice Packet Machine case by the senior managers, in spite of very clear and strong objections of A Van de Clerk, Chief Engineer, Unilever PLC, UK, the Company Secretary, Shyamal Sen and the external lawyer, Sudipto Sarkar. My opinion that we accept the machine and that we can safely handle the remaining problems in India, if needed with Siebler's help, to implement the project was not taken up for consideration, or discussed with me in any manner by K K Nair, or by anyone else, at any time.

A case was promptly filed against Siebler in Kolkata High Court by Brooke Bond Lipton India Ltd. but it has not been pursued seriously till today, obviously because the company knows that it has no strong grounds to win and benefit from the case. Even though I retired about 20 years ago, I think that I should be in the know, if the case was proceeded with, because if any witnesses have to be present in the court for this case, I imagine that I would have to be at least one among them.

Hindustan Lever Ltd. vs. Brooke Bond India Ltd.

It has been reported to me that at the end of an Annual Senior Manager's Conference held in Mumbai, at an open house session of Hindustan Lever Ltd., the year after I retired in 1995, which was attended by P Barua and R Gopalakrishnan sitting at the stage, when a Manager in the audience stood up and raised a question – *"It is the general impression in the open market that Hindustan Lever Ltd. is an arrogant company. What do you have to say to that?"* This question was initially met with a stony silence by all on the stage, for quite a while, until Harish Manwani, the then Chief Operating Officer and non-executive Chairman of Hindustan *Unilever* stood up and responded by saying that – *"I will answer that question, which is that Hindustan Lever is arrogant, because we deserve to be arrogant"*. This, in my personal opinion, has been the basic philosophy of a good number of Leverites, particularly in India, which explains the deep chasm between many employees of Hindustan Unilever Ltd. and Brooke Bond India Ltd. It is really sad to note that a very recent daily newspaper report on the prospective retirement of Manwani that 'Manwani's wise counsel would be personally missed by Unilever CEO Paul Polman, for whom Manwani is both "a friend and a much admired and respected business leader'. In my personal opinion, the trade mark of a typical Hindustan Unilever manager is arrogance and the trade mark of a typical Brooke Bond manager is diagonally the opposite, humility, the culture imbued throughout Brooke Bond when it was controlled by the founding Brooke family members, who were Quakers, who in my opinion are the equivalent of Jains in India.

Approximately Rs. 1,14,00,000/- already spent as out of the total project cost of about Rs. 4,75,00,000/- envisioned in the original Project Proposal has completely gone down the drain, with absolutely no prospect of any salvage, as all the new machinery, equipment, like Siebler Packing Machine, Collator, Gravure Printing, Hot Melt Adhesive Coating, Chilling and Rewinding unit,

Adhesive Testing unit and Packing Machine drawings acquired specifically for this project had to be disposed of at scrap value, or very much less than even its book value, as they could not be put to any other beneficial use anywhere else in Brooke Bond Lipton or in any of the other Unilever factories, elsewhere.

To me the biggest surprise, shock and revelation in this matter is that neither Hindustan Unilever Ltd. in India, nor Unilever PLC, in UK have at any time, till today, probed into this big fiasco, in any way, nor asked me any questions to establish how and who were responsible for and exactly what went wrong to create this big a fiasco. At the same time, I am really happy to say that I have never ever been pointed at, hinted, or accused, at any time, by anyone, including K K Nair, as in anyway responsible for this fiasco.

Clement Wood and his technical innovations.

The only one person I can think of who truly merits a worthwhile mention for any technical contributions to Brooke Bond is Clement Wood, Factory Manager of the Kolkata Factory and Technical Director, Brooke Bond India Ltd. sometime in the late 1920s, or early 1930s, who invented and created some extremely valuable and original technical innovations, over which 6 different Patents (official photo-copies of which are available with me) were granted to him between 1933 and 1936, which in my opinion, paved the way to make Brooke Bond grow to its final big size, overtaking Lipton, which till then was the leader in India.

Talking to several retired executives of Hindustan Unilever Ltd. over the past few months, I was really shocked and dismayed to note that the vast majority of even the long serving engineers, or non-engineers have never even heard of the name Clement Wood, let alone aware of his special, unique and valuable contributions to the company, which sadly reflects on the very poor importance given to engineering and technology by both Brooke Bond and Hindustan Unilever. To those who are concerned or interested about this state of affairs, I suggest that you read what a very large size multi-national company like General Motors, USA does in an identical situation by going through the following two Links in the Internet.

1. http://inventhelp.co.uk/Alfred-Sloans-Concept-of-the-Corporation. asp#.VA2fG8ngWJU, and
2. http://www.autonews.com/article/19970331/ANA/703310750/ boss-kettering-awards-honor-gm-innovators

My engineer son, Ashok Chandy who is a joint holder of 34 Patents and with 3 other Patent applications currently pending approval, spent 10 years with General Motors, 10 years with its spinoff, Delphi and for the last 5 years with Delphi's spinoff, Nexteer, all in the field of Electrical Power Steering of Automobiles and is a winner of the ultimate Boss-Kettering Innovator Award twice and has his portrait permanently displayed in the Innovator's Hall of Fame. It is important to note that the Annual Innovator Awards are given in the name of Boss-Kettering the greatest ever Technical Innovator in the long history of General Motors. I am proud to say that Ashok was invited by Apple in USA to join them in their latest task of working on the design and development of the forthcoming Apple's Autonomous Car.

My post-retirement career.

I am actually extremely happy that I did retire, though prematurely in 1995, because very many favourable circumstances developed in the most unexpected manner around me to continue, immediately after my leaving Brooke Bond Lipton India Ltd., with my retired life with equal zest, energy and fervor and with a wider and interesting variety of technical activities, than before. All these activities are well within my sphere of special interests, which I enjoy working on, giving me not only immense mental, technical and financial satisfaction and rewards, that are way beyond what I might have achieved if I had retired from Brooke Bond Lipton India Ltd., normally at 60 years of age, i.e., two years later. Like the 130+ discoveries, innovations or inventions made by me during my tenure with Brooke Bond India Ltd., and with Brooke Bond Lipton India Ltd., and many more years after my retirement, without making any noise or fanfare, I continue even after taking retirement, with my discoveries, inventions and innovations, at my own comfortable and personal pace and have created several truly original, novel and significant machine designs and development, which can rightly claim several world records.

It is quite interesting to note that all this was achieved by me without the normal head-aches of running a factory of my own, employing anyone as manager, secretary, sales assistant, accountant, engineer, technician, worker, draughtsman, driver, peon, etc., and without going in for any publicity, advertisements, etc., other than my one personal website – www.chandyjohn. com. Even after implementing several ideas, plans, projects, etc., over the immediate past over 20 years, after my retirement, I also have many more new, rich, novel and original ideas rolling in my head now, for future implementation, waiting for a suitable opportunity to take up and start my work on these ideas with other companies. I must admit that I am now receiving many more challenging inquiries than what I can comfortably cope with.

Visit to Moscow.

In this connection, I have to mention the indirect influence of Late V Balaraman, Export Manager, Brooke Bond Lipton India Ltd., had in initiating my new range of post-retirement technical activities. This originates with an endeavor in 1989 by Hindustan Lever Ltd., Mumbai to set up a Tea Blending cum Tea Packing Factory in Moscow, Russia involving Brooke Bond Lipton India Ltd., for providing machineries made by Brooke Bond Lipton India Ltd.'s Development & Machine Building factory at Kolkata, of which I was the head and the inputs of erstwhile Lipton Tea Tasters providing services to buy the required Tea from India and send it to this proposed factory in Moscow and Hindustan Lever Ltd., taking advantage of the export credit in all these transactions, in order to fulfill their export obligations. In that connection, I was selected as an engineer from the Brooke Bond family and a Tea Taster, R B Deane from the Lipton family and V Balaraman from the Hindustan Lever family to make a visit to Moscow for 10 days to meet the Russian team involved and to explore the feasibility of such a venture. This plan was initiated with a joint meeting of all three members of the team in the Mumbai office of R Gopalakrishnan, the then Vice President Exports, Hindustan Lever Ltd., India, where the scope and strategies of this proposed venture were discussed in general. During our stay in Moscow, I had the opportunity of presenting at a meeting of the full Russian and Indian teams, the scope of supply of Machinery from Brooke Bond's Development & Machine Building factory, which I came to know later from V Balaraman, that it did make a very good impact on the Russian Team.

My first post-retirement assignment.

Perhaps, with this old image of me in mind and my current reputation within Brooke Bond Lipton India Ltd., V Balaraman, who is an Accountant, approached me about one week prior to my retirement, i.e., about Aug. 1995, with a technical problem.

V Balaraman explained how Hindustan Lever Ltd., was regularly exporting very expensive Darjeeling Teas to three major Tea companies in Japan, namely, Japan Black Tea, Mitsui and Mitsubishi and all these three Japanese Tea companies considered all these Indian Teas as unfit for public consumption in Japan, when received, as it contained several trace magnetic and non-magnetic impurities heavier than Tea like, Sand, Stones, Mud Balls, small pieces of Glass, Plastic, Iron, Steel, Brass, Copper, Aluminium, Stainless Steel, Iron and Rust Powder and non-magnetic impurities lighter than Tea like, Fiber, Dust, Tea Fluff and Hair (both human and animal). Therefore all these three companies would, on receipt of the Teas in Japan, hand over all the Teas as received, to one of the specialized Cleaning companies, of which there were a total of about 30 to 40 companies, in operation in Japan, around that time. These companies would clean and return the cleaned Teas and also the collected waste impurities, charging the importers US $ 2.00 per Kg of Tea cleaned, for their services. The collected waste impurities regularly had to be exported out of Japan by the respective importers for destruction, as the cost of disposing the same in Japan was more than the cost of exporting the waste out of Japan to any other countries for destruction. V Balaraman said that the Japanese companies were willing to pay Hindustan Lever Ltd. @ US $ 1.00 per Kg of Tea, if the complete work of cleaning the Teas was done in India, before export of the Teas. V Balaraman also mentioned to me that no help in any technical matter related to the Tea Cleaning procedure would be available from Japan, as all the Cleaning companies in Japan were in competition with each other and therefore held the respective processes employed by them as a secret. At the same time neither Unilever in India, UK, or Rotterdam had any technical suggestions or solutions to offer to meet this demand and if I would be in a position to solve this problem in India, he would be most happy. I responded saying, *'give me 2 weeks' time and I'll give you an answer'*. Within 2 weeks, I called Balaraman and said that *'I do have a solution'*, to which he asked whether I can prove it. I offered to prove my claim, if all related expenses were borne by Brooke Bond Lipton India Ltd. This offer was accepted by Balaraman and a 500 Kgs lot of Darjeeling Teas was cleaned under simulated conditions in Bangalore and sent to one of the three clients in Japan for inspection, comments and feedback, which was that "**the Teas are extraordinarily clean**".

So, I was requested to submit a plan to set up a new Plant at Kidderpore, Kolkata to clean 2,000 Kgs of Tea per hour. This plan prepared by me and estimated to cost about Rs. 25,000,000/- was forwarded by Balaraman to R Gopalakrishnan, the then Vice President, Exports, Hindustan Lever Ltd., Mumbai, who commented that everything about the plan was good, except the total estimated cost of Rs. 25,000,000/-, only because this would need approval from Unilever in UK, while a project with an estimated total cost of anything less than Rs. 10,000,000/- could be approved by Hindustan Lever Ltd. in India. Therefore, I was advised to scale down my plan and proposal to a total estimated cost of not more than Rs. 10,000,000/-. Accordingly, I revised the plan for a Plant with a capacity of 600 Kgs per hour and costing less than Rs. 10,000,000/-, which was accepted, approved and implemented in 1996 and is successfully operating at Lipton's old Tea Factory in Kidderpore, Kolkata till today.

Visit to Sri Lanka.

News about the Tea Cleaning project and my involvement in the same not only went to Unilever in UK, but also to Unilever in Sri Lanka. As a result, I was invited in December 1996 by Unilever Ceylon Ltd., – Tea Division., to come to Colombo, study and discuss the feasibility of setting up a much larger capacity Tea Cleaning Plant to be integrated with their two existing Tower type Tea Blending Plants. Sad to say, that the plan developed and submitted by me to Unilever Ceylon never materialised and Brooke Bond Ceylon Ltd., sold their complete Tea Factory including the two Tea Blending Plants, later, to other Sri Lankan Tea companies.

However, that one visit of mine to Colombo eventually led me to land up with four other projects in Sri Lanka and also a fifth project in Jeddah, Saudi Arabia, all of which gave my new retired life an unexpected enormous new thrill, drive, rewards and push.

My assignment with Akbar Brothers Ltd., Sri Lanka.

My first project in Sri Lanka, set up in 1997, was a Tower type Tea Blending Plant of 6 Tons working capacity, for Akbar Brothers Ltd., the No. 1 and by far the biggest dealer and exporter of Teas from Sri Lanka, for a first time ever Tea Blending Machine in the history of this old family owned company. This Plant was set up at their new Tea Blending and Tea Packing factory in Kelaniya, Colombo and continues to work till today, without any problems and to the complete satisfaction of Akbar Brothers.

My assignment with MJF Teas Pvt. Ltd., Sri Lanka.

My second project, set up in 1998, was for the MJF Group, another family owned company, internationally famous for their DILMAH Brand of Teas. MJF set up a 4,000 Kgs per hour continuous type Tea Cleaning Plant integrated with a Tower type Tea Blending Plant of 10 Cubic Meter (4,000 Kgs) working capacity, which can rightly claim a record of being the first of its kind in the world. Today, all Teas blended and packed by MJF are cleaned and blended by this Plant, which is set up in a brand new and very large five storied ultra-modern factory building set up at Peliyagoda, on the immediate outskirts of Colombo. The tall Tower type Tea Blending Plant runs through three floors of this building and continues to work till today, without any major problems and to the complete satisfaction of MJF Group.

My assignment with Jafferjee Brothers Ltd., Sri Lanka.

My third project in Sri Lanka was to set up a Tea Cleaning only unit for Jafferjee Brothers Ltd., Colombo, in 2003, to clean Tea at the rate of 1,500 Kgs per hour.

My project with A M S Baeshen & Co., Jeddah, Saudi Arabia.

My third project, set up in 2000, was for the A M S Baeshen & Co., Jeddah, Saudi Arabia (well known for their RABEA Brand of Teas), a fully Saudi family owned firm, but substantially managed by expatriate managers from UK and all technical staff recruited exclusively from Philippines. This project of mine is truly remarkable in that Baeshen had already with them a complete, and perhaps the then world's most modern (UK made) Drum type Tea Blending Plant designed, made and supplied by UK based, Gordon J Barnes, a world renowned, but now retired expert Tea Blending Machine designer, manufacturer and supplier. Baeshen had grown phenomenally from near zero, since setting up this Plant about 8 years earlier and apart from capturing about 80 % total share of the Saudi domestic Tea market, had a good share of the middle-east Tea market with their RABEA Brand of Teas. Baeshen now wanted to expand and had already approached Gordon J Barnes for the supply and installation of a second Tea Blending Plant of identical capacity, for which Gordon J Barnes initially is reported to have quoted £ 3,500,000/. Even though the basic capacity specified by Baeshen for the proposed new Plant was identical to that of the old and existing Plant, Barnes' new offer was with far-fetched features and at a price that was totally unacceptable even to the cash-rich Baeshen. That was during the period when I was visiting Bede Fernando, the then Managing Director of Van Rees Ceylon Ltd. in Colombo. This order from Baeshen was secured by me, thanks to my personal introduction to the UK expatriate, Shaun Gough, expert Tea Taster and General Manager of Baeshen who was then visiting Van Rees in Colombo and was given a very strong recommendation of me by Bede Fernando.

At that point in time Van Rees Ceylon Ltd. was virtually the exclusive supplier of Sri Lankan Orthodox Teas to Baeshen. I was invited to visit Baeshen's factory, fully at Baeshen's cost, to study and discuss what I could offer. The

Tower type Tea Blending Plant that I was ready to offer was rejected outright because this involved opening up and rebuilding the roof of the Baeshen's fully and centrally air-conditioned large factory in order to accommodate the very tall Tower type Tea Blending Plant that I could offer, which was totally unacceptable to Baeshen. Therefore, I was compelled to replace my offer of the Tower type Tea Blending Plant with a Drum type Tea Blending Plant, very much shorter in height and comparable to the existing Plant supplied by Gordon J Barnes. During my visit to Baeshen's factory and after observing Barnes' Plant in operation, I conveyed to Baeshen that I would be offering a Drum type Tea Blending Plant superior to Barnes' Plant not only in terms of its then certified capacity of 2,021.75 Kgs/Hr., but also in terms of features, performance and specifications, without compromising the quality and performance of my Plant, in any way whatsoever. I also made it quite clear to Baeshen that I cannot specify what would be the exact capacity per hour of my proposed Plant, as I had not manufactured a Drum type Tea Blending Plant till now. Being totally confident in my ability to deliver goods fully, as proposed by me and as required by Baeshen and after negotiating an insignificant price reduction, Baeshen placed the Purchase Order on me, not only to cover the supply of the completely new main Plant, but also to simultaneously supply additional machinery, equipment and accessories required to modify and increase the working capacity of the existing Barnes' old Plant at a total CIF, Jeddah, Saudi Arabia cost of US $ 206,700/. It needs to be mentioned here that Shaun Gough and the UK expatriate Chief Engineer cum Factory Manager, Gordon Sinclair, who took all the key decisions in this matter, had never heard of me earlier, nor seen any of my Plants in operation anywhere, but as verbally explained to me later by Shaun Gough, they were ready to take the risk of ordering the new Plant on me, a totally unknown individual, only because of the high confidence inspired by me in the discussions and at the same time my price was so very attractive, that Baeshen was even fully prepared to scrap my complete new Plant, if by any chance it proved to be a failure later.

According to the terms of the Purchase Order and Letter of Credit, strictly controlled tests were to be carried out on both my newly supplied Plant and the old Barnes' Plant (after increasing its capacity with my upgrades) in order to establish the new capacities available from these two Plants, at maximum dump rate, before releasing the last and final installment of the due payment. The Test Report, copy of which can be seen below, confirming that both Plants

AHMED MOHAMED SALEH BAESHEN & CO.
TEA INDUSTRIES

أحمد محمد صالح باعشن وشركاه
لصناعة الشاي

COMPLETION CERTIFICATE

BLENDING PROJECT HARDWARE INSTALLATION AND COMMISSIONING

PHASE 1

Installation

Equipment	Status
Redoncall Conveyor	Completed
Magnetic Separator	Completed
Screener	Completed
Bucket Elevators	Completed
Blending Drum	Completed
Control Panel	Completed

Performance Trials

Blend	Mix Size (kgs)	Mix Cycle time (min.)	Capacity (kg/Hr)	Capacity/shift
Rabea 315 LL	720	10.75	4018.6	32148.8
All Trading Blds	1334	13.91	5823.65	46589.2

PHASE 2

Installation

Equipment	Status
Redoncall Conveyor	Completed
Magnetic Separator	Completed
Screener	Completed
Control Panel	Completed

Performance Trials

Blend	Mix Size (kg)	Mix Cycle time (min.)	Capacity (kg/Hr)	Capacity/Shift
Rabea 315 LL	720	10.75	4018.6	32148.8
All Trading Blds	1334	13.91	5823.65	46589.2

Total Plant Capacity

Blend	Mix Size (kg)	Mix Cycle time (min.)	Capacity (kg/Hr)	Capacity/Shift
Rabea 315 LL	720	10.75	8037.2	64297.6
All Trading Blds	1334	13.91	11647.3	93178.4

Specification

1. As per the agreed contract between AMSB Baeshen and Chandy John. Blending drum consummeterised volume will be not less than 9.45 Cubic Meters matching the specification of the existing Barnes blending drum.
2. Blending Trials were conducted during the commissioning phase to determine maximum throughput on Phase 1 & Phase 2.
3. Throughput trials were conducted by Chandy John, Gordon Sinclair and Colin Green. Capacities arrived at are at maximum dump speed.
4. Blend trial samples were provided to the Tea Laboratory for analysis and were found to be homogeneous and consistent with our standard pre-blended 315. Rana Generation has indicated that he is satisfied with the blending system performance.

T.I. Factory Manager	Gordon Sinclair
T.I. Senior Tea Buyer	for Rana Generation
Chandy Intertea	Chandy John
T.I. General Manager	Shaun Gough

info@baeshen.com
P.O. BOX 9822, JEDDAH 21423, KINGDOM OF SAUDI ARABIA TEL.: (+966 2)637 9000 FAX: (+966 2) 637 4666 email info@baeshen.com

TOTAL P. 03

gave an exact equal output of 4,018.6 Kgs. /Hr. that measured more than 98 % higher capacity than the original capacity of the old Gordon J Barnes' Plant till it was upgraded by me. I was also verbally informed by Shaun Gough that Gordon Sinclair was deputed to go to UK to negotiate the original quote of Barnes which was reduced after a lot of heavy negotiation from £ 3,500,000 to £ 2,750,000/-. As against this, my combined total package offer, covering the supply of both the complete new machine, together with the supply of additional machinery and accessories required to increase the working capacity of the existing Barnes' Plant amounted to only US $ 206,700/-. The cost of only the completely new Plant (i.e., without the upgrades for the old Plant), in my scope of supply, amounted to only 17 % of the reduced offer of £

2,750,000/- by Barnes, while giving me and also all my associated Vendors very attractive and sufficiently satisfying profits.

Though it is very understandable if all these statements of mine would sound very strange and unbelievable to most readers, I have with me all the documents, quotations, test certificates, testimonials, etc., to prove all my above mentioned statements, prices and the increase in working capacities obtained from both Plants, but unfortunately I have only a verbal statement of Shaun Gough, regarding Barnes' quoted prices. In spite of my repeated entreaties, Shaun Gough stubbornly refused to give me a full photocopy of Barnes' first, or the revised quote, even after the complete capacity tests on the two Plants confirmed the above mentioned output per Hour. It was self-evident to me that Shaun Gough was refusing to give me a full photocopy of Barnes' first, or even the revised quote, only because, it would really be very embarrassing to Shaun Gough for any outsider to see that Baeshen was almost going to be conned in a very big way by Barnes, before I came into the picture. However, I have a photo-copy of Barnes' original quote, with all prices blanked out, which was given to me by Baeshen, at a very early stage in our negotiations to help me prepare my quote in a manner that would be easy for Baeshen to make side-by-side comparisons between the two offers. This Plant continues to work till today, without any problems and to the complete satisfaction of Baeshen. It must also be mentioned that the quality of my supply of machineries and equipment was in no way inferior to and was on par with the quality of all machinery and equipment supplies made by Barnes from UK.

Assignment with Jafferjee Brothers Ltd., Sri Lanka.

My fourth project, set up in 2003, was to set up a stand-alone Tea Cleaning Plant of 1,500 Kgs per Hour capacity for Jafferjee Brothers Ltd., Colombo, Sri Lanka.

Project with Van Rees Ceylon Ltd., Sri Lanka.

My fifth project, set up in 2006, was for Van Rees Ceylon Ltd. the largest division of the Dutch multi-national, Van Rees B V, The Netherlands, the world's largest independent Tea dealer cum Tea supplier. By independent, it is meant that Van Rees do not have any Brands of their own, but they purchase / blend and pack teas on behalf other Brand owners in different parts of the world. The success of these Brands by the respective Brand owners would be a success story for Van Rees. Hence the need to provide its customers with a high-hygiene product, un-touched by human hands, which was of paramount importance at the time this ground breaking project was initiated. Until the time this project of mine was executed and commissioned in Colombo, all long leafy Orthodox type Ceylon Teas were blended and packed by Van Rees Ceylon manually on the floor, right from the company's inception in Sri Lanka and for some decades, only because no machine was known to be able to handle these extraordinarily long, twisted and wiry Teas, because of its very poor flow characteristics.

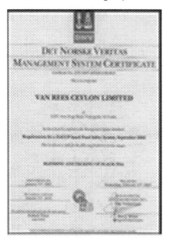

When this new project was fully implemented in 2006, Van Rees Ceylon Ltd. had a 7,000 Kgs per Hour continuous type Tea Cleaning Plant, integrated with a batch and Drum type Tea Blending Plant of 8,400 Liters working capacity, or 21,000 Liters total Internal Volume, which is believed to be the largest Drum type Tea Blending Unit in the world. This Plant has also been officially certified as HACCP Compliant as can be seen in the photocopy of the Certificate shown here. Today, all Teas blended and packed by Van Rees Ceylon Ltd. are completely cleaned and blended by this Plant, which continues to work till today, without any problems and to the complete satisfaction of Van Rees. To the best of my belief and as on 2006, this Plant can rightly claim six different world records, as follows: -

1. The world's first (7,000 Kgs per hour) Tea Cleaning Plant integrated with a Drum type Tea Blending Plant of 8,400 Liters working capacity.

2. The world's first large scale Tea Blending Plant that can comfortably accept and handle a batch size of 1,500 Kgs of the very largest Leaf Ceylon Orthodox type Teas like, OPA, OP1 and OP grade Teas, having Bulk Densities in the range of 5.7 Liters per Kg, or more without any difficulty or problems. These Teas are normally difficult and problematic to work with, because of its very poor Flow Characteristics and therefore traditionally handled only by blending manually on the floor.

3. To the best of my knowledge this 8,400 Liters working capacity (21,000 Liters total internal volume) Drum type Blending Plant has, to the best of my knowledge, the largest Blending Drum used for blending Teas anywhere in the world.

4. It is generally and commonly opined in the Tea trade that no Tea Blending Machine can deliver results comparable to a properly managed manual blending operation of the same Teas on the floor. To the best of my knowledge, this is the first time that any reputed Tea Expert (of Van Rees Ceylon Ltd. who had several decades of experience in manual blending of Teas on the floor) has certified, in writing, that the results of blending Teas on this Plant offers results that are superior to the results of manual blending of the same Teas on the floor, in respect of the following: -

    a. The degree of uniformity of mix through the whole batch of any Teas blended in this Plant is superior to the degree of uniformity of mix through the whole batch of any Teas of the same type and grade of Teas, if manually blended on the floor.

    b. The breakage of even the most delicate and highly friable very large Leaf Orthodox type and OPA, OP1 and OP grade Teas blended in this Plant is less than the breakage of the same type and grade of Teas, if manually blended on the floor.

c.   The loss of Bloom (or Greying) of any Teas blended in this Plant is less than the loss of Bloom of the same type and grade of Teas, if manually blended on the floor.

As no large size Drum type Tea Blending Plant capable of accepting and working with the delicate and highly friable very large Leaf Ceylon Orthodox type OPA, OP1 and OP grade Teas was known to exist, or proven to work without damaging these Teas in any way, I put forward a condition that I would undertake this work only if about 2,000 Kgs of the very large Leaf Ceylon Orthodox type OPA Teas were delivered to me in Bangalore, free of all costs, to carry out the tests and trials required to establish a procedure and plan to develop a suitable machine. Only after carrying out several tests and trials over a six month period, was I able to confirm feasibility of delivering such a Plant and give a green signal to Van Rees to go ahead and place the Purchase Order, pay the Advance Payment and open the Letter of Credit.

My International Travels.

I have travelled, with my wife, to 56 different countries once, 19 countries twice, and 2 countries 5 and 11 times respectively, covering all our expenses from my own pocket for all these travels, except for travels to 10 countries once each, on official trips.

I have fully paid up for a totally new 1,350 Sq. Ft. 2-bedroomed apartment in a very modern and dedicated Senior Citizen's Home, in Whitefield and taken full possession of by me. Over and above this, I have managed to multiply the total liquid assets that I had at the time of taking Voluntary Retirement, by several times, through the span of about 20 years after my retirement. Over and above this, I have a sufficiently reasonable financial backup to meet all foreseeable needs, till the end of our two lives. All this was made possible, entirely from my own earnings, after retirement.

I am sure that K K Nair cannot read this long document fully, as he has very often mentioned to me that any letter, note or article written by me in more than two pages will go straight into his waste paper basket. Apart from that, I seriously doubt if he, as my boss for 8 years, is even remotely aware of even 10 % of my 130+ achievements listed under Annexure A in this note.

K K Nair's impact on my personal contributions and achievements, while working under him for 8 years in Brookefields, Bangalore, towards the very end of my career with Brooke Bond Lipton India Ltd. can be gauged from the list of my achievements while in Brookefields working under him for 8 years, compared with the list of my achievements while working under 14 other different bosses in my entire 58 year career, which I can recollect as of now and are as listed below: -

Annexure A

List of my significant and note-worthy achievements over the immediate past 58 years, (including 21 years after my retirement in Sept. 1995) and the Plans I now have, ready for implementation in future.

While at the National Tobacco Cigarette Factory, Kolkata, 1961 to 1963.

As Maintenance Engineer, I concentrated primarily on the entire fleet of about 28 Molins' Cigarette Making Machines, which had the most severe problems amongst all the different types of machines working in the whole factory, I had the golden opportunity to watch and study the complete over-hauling process of some 10 Cigarette Making Machines, done by one expert Engineer, deputed solely for this purpose from Molins Tobacco Machinery Co., UK, who had manufactured and supplied all the Molins Cigarette Making Machines installed in the factory. This engineer had agreed to undertake overhaul of only the 10 newest Molins' Cigarette Making machines in the factory and refused to have anything to do with any of the other 18 older Molins Cigarette Making machines, saying that they should be condemned, discarded and replaced with new machines.

After this Molins Engineer completed his committed work and left India for UK, I took over the task of overhauling all the remaining 18 older Molins' Cigarette Making machines rejected by the visiting Molins Engineer. I am glad to say that the management of National Tobacco Co. of India Ltd. was extremely happy that I completed the task of overhauling all the remaining 18 Cigarette Making Machines in about 15/18 months and I was also able to obtain performances from all these 18 old machines, absolutely on par with the performances of all the 10 much newer machines, all of which were only recently overhauled by the visiting Molins' UK Engineer.

While at Brooke Bond's Hide Rd, Kolkata Factory, 1963 to 1972.

1. My first major task here was to completely shift all the existing machines, furniture and fittings in the narrow and cramped hall, at the very extreme rear end corner of the factory to a more spacious and more conveniently located hall almost in the center of the factory.

2. Over a period of time, rescued all the infamous 27 UK designed, but Brooke Bond India Ltd. made Berkshire Gravure Printing cum Bag Making Machines installed in the 6 Tea factories of Brooke Bond India Ltd. all over India, from an ignominious reputation as the most trouble making group of machines in the entire history of Brooke Bond in India, into a very highly reliable and virtually trouble free machine, which helped to enhance the availability of high quality Pice Packet Paper Bags to fully and reliably meet the very large market demands of Tea Pice Packets all over India.

3. Invented a remarkably simple and inexpensive technique of employing a Trammel like arrangement, in conjunction with an imported ultra-precision (± 0.001 inch over 24 inches) Spirit Level for measuring, adjusting and setting the parallelism and perpendicularity of any number of Shafts, or Rollers placed at relatively large distances from each other and far beyond the reach of any commercially available, Micrometer, or Vernier Calipers. This simple and very cheap tool played a very crucial role in debugging one of the main operating problems of all the Berkshire Gravure Printing & Bag Making Machines and was significantly superior to an equivalent gadget / arrangement (fitted with a Dial Micrometer), that I have seen used by Bobst, Switzerland, the world's premier Gravure Printing Machine manufacturer and renowned Gravure Printing Machine manufacturer, for the very same purpose. This serves as a good and proper alternative means of achieving parallelism of Shafts at long distances from each other, easily and with a very high degree of accuracy and which can normally be matched and set with the help of only sophisticated and very expensive imported Optical Auto-Collimators, which costs over Rs. 30,00,000/- for a set. To the best of my knowledge, there are very few organizations in India (Hindustan Aeronautics Ltd. is one) equipped with Optical Auto-Collimators to implement such a task in India.

4. Modified the existing original UK designed Berkshire 2-lane Gravure Printing cum Paper Bag Making Machines to a 3-lane Printing cum Paper Bag Making Machine, for the very first time in Brooke Bond India Ltd. and anywhere in India, thereby increasing the productivity of these machines by 50 %, while employing the same machine and manpower. This made it possible to completely do away with the entire fleet of 10 lower output, imported Strachan & Henshaw Automatic Paper Bag Making Machines, which had no printing facilities and therefore had to depend on outside Printing Presses for the supply of Printed Paper Rolls to make Paper Bags on these Strachan & Henshaw Paper Bag Making Machines and meeting future growth requirements of Pice Packet Bags solely by the productivity increase of the existing Berkshire Gravure Printing cum Paper Bag Making Machines and without addition of any more machines or manpower.

5. Invented, designed and introduced the concept of integrating the Drive Shaft and Gravure Cylinder, replacing all the original UK designed multi-piece Sleeve-and-Shaft type Gravure Cylinders. Along with this, a totally new integrated Ball and Roller Bearings supported (replacing all the original UK designed Bush Bearing supported) Gravure Cylinder & Mandrel assemblies that made it possible to very significantly increase the working life, improve the print quality obtained from Gravure Cylinders, reduce Paper and Ink Spoils, on all 27 + 3 = 30 Berkshire type Gravure Printing Machines used in India by a very big margin and also greatly simplify machine adjustments and operation.

6. Designed and introduced a totally new Ball and Roller Bearing supported (replacing all the original UK designed Bush Bearing supported) Impression Roller Assembly that made it possible to greatly increase the working life of Rubber Impression Rollers and print quality of Gravure Cylinders and also reduce Paper and Ink Spoils by a significant margin.

7. Introduced a new method of mounting worn Rubber Lined Impression Rollers on a Mandrel and then regrinding the Rubber surface with the Mandrel mounted center to center on a Lathe, in order to ensure perfect concentricity of the outside ground surface of the Rubberized Impression Rollers with respect to the imaginary and true center-line of the Impression Roller Ball Bearing centers. This made it possible to

greatly increase the working life of all the Rubber Impression Rollers, improve print quality of Gravure Cylinders and also reduce Paper and Ink Spoils by a big margin.

8. Introduced the concept of using Print Register Marks as useful and visible cues for ease of controlling the Print Register, Cutting and Folding of Bags and Flats more effectively, for the very first time in Brooke Bond India Ltd.

9. Introduced the concept of a novel and safer Electrical Wiring for all the 30 Berkshire type Gravure Printing Machines working all over India, as a very economical and practical substitute for the very much more expensive Flame Proof Electrical Wiring and Accessories. This concept virtually eliminated the Electrical Fires, which were an occasional occurrence earlier, all over Brooke Bond India Ltd.'s factories. This is of considerable importance, because large quantities of highly volatile and inflammable solvents like Toluene and Xylene are not only used in the various Printing Units of each Gravure Printing Machines, but also stored in several large 200 Liter Drums in the printing department. Even though several fires have occurred in the past, to the best of my knowledge, there has never been any instance of even a petty fire in any of the Berkshire type Gravure Printing Machines since this concept of mine was introduced all over India on all the Berkshire type Gravure Printing Machines employed in Brooke Bond India Ltd.

10. Introduced the concept of fully Side-Seam type of Paper Bag Formation, probably for the very first time in India, to replace the original and universally followed Center-Seam type Paper Bag Formation, adopted not only by Brooke Bond India Ltd. throughout India and possibly elsewhere, till that point in time. This is now virtually a standard type of Paper Bag Formation adopted by nearly all Converters throughout India, which offers an equally large Panel area for Printing on both sides of the Paper Bag, thereby making it possible to have an identical and larger printed Panel display on both sides of Pice Packets.

11. Reduced the width of the Side-Seam from 19 mm to 12.5 mm, the width of the Bottom Fold, from 19 mm to 12.5 MM, width of the Top Fold, from 19 mm to 12.5 MM, of all Pice Packets produced by Brooke Bond India Ltd. all over India, thereby reducing the total Paper consumption, without reducing the front and back Panel sizes or print area available for printing of all Pice Packets. The above mentioned

three modifications to the construction and style of Pice Packet Bags not only contributed a total and permanent reduction in consumption of Paper by 27.3 % and at the same time made the Packet aesthetically more attractive, offering a much larger printed display panel on both sides of the Packet.

12. Designed and introduced a simple and cheap Web Breakage Detector for automatically stopping the Berkshire type Gravure Printing Machines instantly, in the event of a Web Breakage, for the very first time in Brooke Bond India Ltd., thereby helping to reduce not only Paper and Ink spoils, but also reduce time required for cleanup and re-starting the machine after every instance of web breakage.

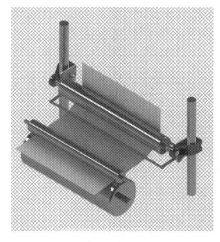

13. Introduced the concept of using a variable Electronic Stroboscope for the purpose of checking the smooth rotary performance of any high speed machine running with any type of Gears, to identify the inherent source of the problem of erratic rotary performance, for the very first time in Brooke Bond India Ltd. and possibly in India. The defects in rotational motion caused by badly machined Gears can easily be detected by employing a variable Stroboscope, which was used to locate the exact sources in the machine causing length variation in Pice Packet Bags during its manufacture and consequent running problems in all the 122 Pice Packet Tea Filling & Packing Machines operating in India.

14. Introduced the concept and implemented an indigenous fully Automatic Pneumatic Web Tension Controller, for the first-time-in-India, in co-operation with M/s Mahindra Electronics, Kolkata with a view to maintain the tension in the Paper Web constant and thereby reduce frequency of web breakage and also maintain steady Print Register Control. One Gravure Printing Machine equipped with this Automatic Pneumatic Web Tension Controller was made and sold to Sigma Inc., Kolkata.

15. Modified one existing original UK designed Berkshire type three-colour Gravure Printing cum Sheet Cutting Machine to a four-colour Machine, thereby making it possible to print by Gravure and produce in-house superior quality and cheaper A-1 Dust 25 and 50 Grams four-colour Flats, for the very first time in Brooke Bond India Ltd. and permanently doing away with printing of the same by outside commercial printers.

16. Designed and developed a very simple, cheap, totally indigenous and patentable automatic electronic Photocell based Web Guiding Device for the Berkshire Gravure Flat Printing and Sheet Cutting Machine to help produce Flats of consistently uniform width, thereby helping to reduce  Paper and Ink spoils at the time of Flat printing and manufacture and during subsequent Packing operations.

17. Invented, designed and made a Gear motor driven patentable Paper Reel Lifting and manual Reel Changing Device, for the very first time in Brooke Bond India Ltd. and in India that totally eliminated the need to manually lift and place heavy Paper Reels on the Reel Carrier Stand of the Berkshire Printing Machines, thereby helping to reduce the risk of Spinal injuries to workers. This device was a remarkably cheap substitute for the very much more expensive fully automatic Reel Splicing and Change-over Unit used in nearly all high-speed Web-based Printing Machines throughout the world.

    News of this creation and achievement of results reached Brooke Bond, UK that Mr. David Brooke, an Engineer, Director and one of the Brooke family members who controlled Brooke Bond UK, made a special appointment to see an actual and complete demonstration of how this end result was made possible by such a cheap and simple device, during one of his visits to the Kolkata Factory.

18. Invented, designed and got made a special purpose light, portable and cheap Wooden Ramp with which the machine operator rolled and mounted a Paper Reel weighing about 100 Kgs onto the Berkshire

Machines Reel Stand, with little effort. Until then, it was necessary for two workers to simultaneously lift the same Reel from the ground and mount the Paper Reel onto the Machine's Reel Stand.

19. Introduced the concept of buying Master Reels of over 1,000 mm Reel Widths through Tea Movement Warehouse and slitting these Reels to various smaller widths to meet the different in-house requirements, for the very first time in Brooke Bond India Ltd. thereby reducing the net purchase price per Kg., of the same Paper and also reduce the quantity of buffer stock of different slit and ready to use Paper Reels required for different applications in the company.

20. Introduced an Electric Overhead Travelling Crane that helped eliminate the heavy and difficult manual work of lifting and loading the heavy and over 1,000 mm wide Master Reels, weighing about 300+ Kgs and also lifting and removing the Slit Reels from the three Chambon Master Reel Slitting Machines, for the very first time in Brooke Bond India Ltd.

21. Introduced Stainless Steel Paster Wheels and Spindles, replacing the original UK designed Brass Paster Wheels and Brass Spindles, thereby significantly improving the quality of Paste application on Pice Packet Bags, by a very big margin and also increasing the life of Paster Wheels.

22. Modified the Cutting Unit of two imported Chambon 2-colour Gravure Printing Machines to produce more than 10,00,000 End Labels per shift, per machine, each of 35 X 25 mm Postage Stamp like size, in 10 lanes and fully finished, to meet the complete requirements of all the Hesser and CRP Packing Machines working with Brooke Bond in India, for the very first time, thereby completely doing away with the old costlier practice of getting the Labels printed by outside commercial Printers.

23. Invented, designed and got made a totally new Slitting Knife Holder Assembly that totally eliminated the need to reset the combination of Spacers of different widths placed between adjacent Slitting Knife Holder Assemblies, every time the Slitting Knife was removed and replaced after grinding, for sharpening of its edges, thereby ensuring Reels to be slit to a very high degree of precision of Reel Width, quickly and repeatedly on all the three imported Chambon Reel Slitting Machines, for the very first time in Brooke Bond India Ltd.

24. Adopted a variation of the above mentioned Slitting Knife Holder Assembly that totally eliminated the need to reset the combined set of Spacers between adjacent Slitting Knife Holder Assemblies, every time the Slitting Knife was removed and replaced after grinding, for sharpening of its edges when the Knife was blunted, thereby ensuring slitting of all End Labels produced on the imported Chambon Gravure Label Printing Machines to a very high order of precision and accuracy from all the 10 Rows, at all times.

25. Introduced for the first time in India an imported UK made Crossfield HELIOSTAT, an electrostatic Gravure Ink Pick-Up Assist Unit, to improve quality of Gravure Prints. Though the unit showed some improved results in printing, the project was abandoned as the extent of print quality improvement achieved was limited and did not warrant the high cost of the imported unit.

26. Imported for the first time in India, a special purpose custom-made German SCHOBER Rotary Hole Punching Device which was fitted to a Brooke Bond India Ltd. made Berkshire type Reel to Reel Gravure Printing Machine, to produce register printed and hole-punched Tags, for the very first time in India, as required for use on all IMA Tea Bag Packing Machines in use with Brooke Bond in India. Prior to this, printed and punched Tag Paper Rolls were imported from Sri Lanka, as there was no one in India capable of producing such Tag Paper Reels.

27. Introduced possibly for the first time in India, an imported Pin Cushion Dot Screen, for etching Gravure Cylinders, which not only helped substantially increase life of all Gravure Cylinders used in Brooke Bond India Ltd. but also helped increase the market share in the sale of Gravure Cylinders made and sold by Brooke Bond India Ltd. to outside customers in India and abroad.

28. Introduced for the very first time in Brooke Bond India Ltd., a very simple and cheap modification to the Ink Storage Tanks of all Gravure Printing Machines, reversing the connection of the Ink Drainage Pipes to the Ink Storage Tanks from Female/Male to Male/Female, which virtually eliminated the possibility of the connection getting accidentally separated and Ink spilling on to the ground, which was a fairly frequent occurrence.

29. Experimented successfully with the concept of Water-Based (instead of Solvent-Based) Gravure Printing Inks, but had to abandon the same on account of higher basic cost of Water-Based Inks.

30. Introduced the concept and routine practice of Testing of all supplies of Gravure Printing Inks and Gravure Solvents at all factories in Brooke Bond India Ltd. for Quality Control of Gravure Printing Inks and Gravure Solvents, for the very first time in Brooke Bond India Ltd. This helped to keep a check on the quality of supplies of all Gravure Printing Inks and also eliminate to the possibility of adulterating the Gravure Solvents and simultaneously obtain maximum mileage from the expensive Gravure Printing Inks and improve Print Quality.

31. Introduced the practice of mixing cheap cooked Tapioca Powder Paste with different types of expensive synthetic Adhesives, used for different applications, thereby not only reducing overall costs, at the same time, making a significant improvement to the performance of Adhesives on the Packing Machines and Packing Benches, for the very first time in Brooke Bond India Ltd.

32. Introduced the practice of adding a small dose of colour Dye to Adhesives, which otherwise are near transparent and consequently not easily visible to the naked Eye on high-speed machines, for the very first time in Brooke Bond India Ltd. and therefore difficult to control and adjust the application of such near transparent Adhesives. This procedure helped operators to easily see and adjust the correct quantity and location of Adhesives applied to Packets or Bags, thereby improving the control and consequently the quality of Paste application in all automatic machines.

33. Introduced and developed all necessary arrangements for manually manufacturing of cheap Pitch Kraft Containers (**PKC**s) by Contractors to replace the more expensive Plywood and Wood Boxes, used to pack Tea and Coffee Packets, for the very first time in Brooke Bond India Ltd.

34. Introduced the concept of making and using Jigs and Fixtures in the manufacture of new Parts and Spare Parts for Machines, for the very first time in Brooke Bond India Ltd., thereby greatly helping to improve the time required to replace the old and worn out parts and to achieve quick, easy and total interchangeability of old and worn out parts with new parts and thereby not only help improve the working

life of parts but also the performance of the machines to which these parts are fitted.

35. Introduced the concept of using Hobbed Spur, Helical Gears and Generated Bevel Gears, for the very first time, for Machines manufactured by Brooke Bond India Ltd., thereby elevating the overall quality and performance level of Brooke Bond India Ltd., made Machines by a very significant margin. Simultaneously, nearly all Gear Holes Centers were reset on machines to be within the strict tolerances required for these gears, in order to get the full benefit of the new higher quality Gears.

36. Modified the original four-Belt Packet Feed and Delivery arrangement of the original Woods Pice Packet Machine all over India to a two-Belt Packet Feed and Delivery arrangement thereby helping to make the whole Machine shorter in length by about 50 %, compact and more efficient, for the very first time in Brooke Bond India Ltd. Simultaneously, the Main Drive arrangement below the Machine Table was also modified and simplified, which helped keep the surroundings and below-the-machine floor area clean and to reduce Tea wastage.

37. Introduced the concept of total overhauling of Tea Packing Machines, in 1964 for the very first time ever in Brooke Bond India Ltd. Until then, these machines were maintained only by ad-hoc repair work. Tom Harris, the expatriate Assistant Factory Manager took a lot of convincing from me, before he would agree to release machines in rotation, for periods of 4 to 6 weeks each, in order to carry out the total overhauling work. The benefit of introducing this practice proved itself in due course of time, that gradually this became an established practice in all the other Brooke Bond factories in India.

38. Introduced for the very first time in Brooke Bond India Ltd. a Production based Incentive Scheme for Fitters at the Kolkata factory that helped to motivate the fitters to partake in the efforts of machine operators to maximize production from machines.

39. Introduced for the very first time in Brooke Bond India Ltd. in India the concept and application of Tolerances in Engineering Drawings.

40. Introduced for the very first time in Brooke Bond India Ltd. in India the use and application of GO / NO GO Plug Gauges for the quick and easy inspection of the accuracy of the new spare parts to machines.

41. Introduced successfully for the very first time in Brooke Bond India Ltd. in India, the practice of getting a few critical Cams for the CRP Packing Machines manufactured at Hindustan Lever Ltd.'s Kolhapur Machine Building Factory, using Computer Aided Design, with a view to improve the performance of the CRP Packing Machines.

42. Introduced for the very first time in Brooke Bond India Ltd., the application and use of Sintered Phosphor Bronze and Sintered Cast Iron Bushes, which are not only functionally superior and longer lasting, but also much more economical and convenient to use, by making possible replacements very quick and easy.

43. Introduced hardened and tempered thick Spring Steel Plates to manufacture Former Plates and Tear-Off Plates replacing the previous Mild Steel Plates which greatly enhanced the life of both Plates by a significant margin.

44. Designed, got manufactured and introduced Electrical Motor driven Bulk Density Meters for the very first time in the 1960s, in Brooke Bond India Ltd. that helped to replace all the imported hand operated Bulk Density Meters, thereby greatly helping to make its operation to measure Bulk Density of different types and grades of Teas, simpler, faster, more reliable and repeatable. Over a period of two years all the imported hand operated Bulk Density Meters in use all over India were scrapped and replaced by Motor driven Bulk Density Meters, made under my guidance by a local Vendor. According to the last information available with me a total of 75 such Bulk Density Meters are in use with Brooke Bond Lipton India Ltd. in Sale Rooms, Factories and Quality Control Laboratories.

While at Brooke Bond's Coimbatore Factory, 1972 to 1979.

45. Introduced four German designed and John Fowler India Ltd., Bangalore made Eirich Mills (one in Coimbatore, one in Ghatkesar and two in Tea Movements Warehouse, Kolkata), for size reduction of original Tea particles, for the very first time in Brooke Bond India Ltd., or anywhere in India. Eventually the four Eirich Mills completely replaced all the original Wood's Tea size reduction machines, running in different Brooke Bond India Ltd. factories in India for decades, which required a large number of men for operation, occupied a lot

of floor space and gave low output. The particle size reduction of original Teas contributed huge savings in Tea cost, over the several years when it was in use by reducing the particle size of Original Teas of large particle sizes, which were available at attractive prices in the Tea Auctions and then mixing the size reduced Teas with similarly sized original Teas of smaller particle sizes, which are more in demand and consequently fetch higher prices. This practice of Tea Particle size reduction which had contributed to really huge savings in the purchase cost of Teas over several decades of operation has now been completely stopped, due to change in Tea market conditions, whereby such cheaper Teas are no longer available in the market.

46. Introduced a 15 inch diameter Double Drum Ferrite Magnetic Separators, with Greenwald-Buss Magnet configuration inside the Drum, at Coimbatore factory for the very first time in the Tea industry in India, thereby paving the way for assured compliance of Prevention of Food Adulteration Act in respect of maximum permitted Iron Particles in Tea @ 250 PPM, for all Teas sold by Brooke Bond India Ltd. throughout India. This unit was subsequently introduced for all the other six Brooke Bond Tower type Tea Blenders in the other Tea Factories of Brooke Bond India Ltd. in India. Currently Hindustan Unilever Ltd. openly touts the superiority of Hindustan Unilever Ltd.'s packed Teas as having much less impurities in the form of Iron Particles in Tea, compared to the Teas sold by virtually all competitors in India, which can be solely attributed to these 15 inch diameter Double Drum Ferrite Magnetic Separators, for which I can take all credit. Please see Page 4 of The Hindustan Lever House Magazine, 'Hamara' of January / February 2003, to read the claims made by Hindustan Lever Ltd. in this regard.

47. Introduced a 15 inches diameter Triple Drum Ferrite Magnetic Separator, with Greenwald-Buss Magnet configuration inside the Drum, for the first time in the Tea industry in India, for total compliance of maximum permitted Iron Particles in Tea @ 150 PPM, for all Teas exported by Brooke Bond India Ltd. to Egypt.

48. Introduced a large 3.65 Meter long X 0.75 Meter wide single-deck horizontally reciprocating rectangular and counterbalanced Vibratory Sifter (of Vokes Cardwell, UK design, but manufactured by John Fowler India Ltd., Bangalore), for the very first time in Brooke Bond

India Ltd. to replace the old and distressingly inefficient Manual Sorting Band of the Brooke Bond Tower type Tea Blender in Coimbatore factory and subsequently for all the other six Brooke Bond Tower type Tea Blenders in use by Brooke Bond India Ltd. in India. This made totally redundant the need for the two workers constantly engaged, one on each side of the Sorting Band to manually pick and remove the larger impurities in Teas. It also helped very greatly improve the efficiency of separating and removing both large and small impurities in Teas by a very big margin.

49. Invented, designed, developed and got manufactured 127 Nos. modified 15-Head Tea Filling Turret assemblies, which replaced the original old erratic and inefficient 10-Head Filling Turret assemblies of the original  127 existing Woods Pice Packet Machines then in operation throughout India. This helped to improve Tea Filling accuracy and repeatability and also uniformity and consistency of Top Folding and Sealing of Pice Packets to a very great extent. The design and process of manufacture of the 15-Head Tea Filling Turrets is a truly remarkable technical achievement, in that it required only the use of simple and cheap Lathes and Milling Machines available at any common and average Machine Shop to manufacture all the individual machine components required to achieve the same end result of the performance of the Pice Packet Tea Filling, Bag Folding and Creasing Process that would be possible using expensive high-precision Jig Boring Machines.

50. Invented, designed, developed and manufactured an ultra-compact Pice Packet Machine with a totally new Volumetric Cup Filler and wBag Pick-Up Funnels that were capable of filling not only the easy and free flowing Tea into Pice Packets with a much higher

order of Weight Accuracy and also fill Coffee and Chicory Powder Mixture, which has very poor flow characteristics, with fairly uniform and acceptable accuracy. This modification of the Pice Packet Packing Machine transformed the original very simple and ungainly Wood's Pice Packet Packing Machine into a precision Packing Machine.

51. Designed a totally new and original concept Magnetic Separator for separating and removing all traces of Iron and Rust Particles from Tea going in to fill Pice Packets, at an extraordinarily high level of Iron separating efficiency. I am now in a position to improve on the level of this Iron separating efficiency further by an even greater margin.

52. Invented, designed, developed and got manufactured a simple, cheap, totally new and original concept Tea Packet Shredding Machine, for  the very first time in Brooke Bond India Ltd. to enable recovery of Tea from damaged or defective Tea Packets at an extra-ordinary high rate of throughput and capable of being managed by only two workers. This machine was made and supplied from Coimbatore to all the other 5 Brooke Bond India Ltd.'s Tea Packing factories in India, for use in salvaging of Tea from damaged packets, resulting in a huge reduction of man-power previously engaged in manual salvaging of Tea from individual defective Packets at all Brooke Bond India Ltd. factories.

53. Introduced the concept of a centralized Tea Dust Collection System to collect Tea Dust released into the atmosphere at various points from all Tea Packing Machines by suction, thereby not only helping to reduce Air Pollution and damage to machines, but also virtually helping to eliminate the largest single source of loss of Tea at Coimbatore factory. The collected Tea Dust was automatically fed back into the bulk Tea when blending Tea, in a controlled manner, for the very first time in Brooke Bond India Ltd. thereby totally salvaging the entire collection of Tea Dust and also totally eliminating the need for manual labour required for denaturing the collected Tea Waste, under direct personal supervision by a Central Excise Officer, prior to sale of the denatured Tea either for manufacture of Caffeine by Pharmaceutical Companies, or for sale to Farmers for use as Fertiliser.

54. Introduced the concept of Suction retrieval of residual Tea from Empty Tea Chests to extract the last small traces of Tea left behind in Tea Chests, after the contents of bulk Tea has been emptied into the In-Feed Hopper of the Tea Blending Machine, for the very first time in Brooke Bond India Ltd.

55. Instrumental in increasing the speed of all CRP Tea Packing Machines operating all over India by 25 %, i.e., from 60 Packets per minute to 75 Packets per minute, for the very first time in Brooke Bond India Ltd. engaging the same existing number of workers per machine.

56. Instrumental in obtaining an increase in output of nearly all Hand-Packing Benches in both Tea and Coffee Factory in Coimbatore by about 25 %.

57. Instrumental in progressively increasing the speed of all the 127 Wood's Pice Packet Tea Fill- Seal Machines running in all 6 Tea factories in India, from 90 Packets per minute in the late 1960s, first to 120, then to 150, then to 200 and then finally to 220 Packets per minute in the 1970s, thereby increasing its total productivity by over 144 %, using the existing number of workers per machine, all with my initiative and during my tenure in the company.

58. Instrumental in increasing the speed of all Dilkush Coffee/Chicory Tableting Machines in India by 50 %, i.e., from 60 to 90 Tablets per minute, for the very first time in Brooke Bond India Ltd. engaging the same existing number of workers per machine.

59. Modified the basic structure of complete fleet of 12 Dilkush Coffee Tableting Machines at Coimbatore, to reduce its foot-print by nearly 50 %, thereby reducing floor space required by these fleet of machines in the factory by a big margin and simultaneously making the Main Machine Drive simpler, more direct and robust.

60. Introduced the concept of periodic Aerosol spraying of Silicone Fluid on to the outer front faces of the Upper and Lower Punches of the Dilkush Coffee/Chicory Powder Tableting Machine, in order to reduce the frequency and intensity of the Coffee/Chicory Powder mixture getting adhered to the faces of the Punches and thereby disfiguring the Tablets, for the very first time in Brooke Bond India Ltd.

61. Invented, designed and got made a patentable system of Closed Loop Air Conveying and Cooling of Coffee Powder, instantly after grinding the Roasted Coffee Beans, by means of cold Air, and at the same

time without any loss of Coffee Flavour. This was first introduced at Ghatkesar Factory, instead of at Coimbatore Factory, as Coimbatore Factory lacked the facility for continuous cooling of the hot Air generated in the system, which required a fairly large quantity of re-circulating cold water for this operation.

62. Invented, designed and got made totally new and original, Turret type automatic Bag Sealing cum Bag Trimming Machines to pack Green Label Coffee Powderin 250g, 500g and 1kg Duplex Polyethylene Gusseted Bags, manually packed on Hand Packing Benches at Coimbatore and Ghatkesar factories.

63. Conceptualised (but never got around to implementing) a very interesting plan to extract pure and natural Coffee Flavour from Roasted and Ground Coffee Beans (by a process linked to the plan of Air Cooling of Coffee Powder) that could have revolutionized Instant Coffee Quality, if it was properly implemented. Unfortunately, I never worked in an Instant Coffee manufacturing factory to implement, test and prove the workability of this plan.

64. Introduced a change in production procedure and plan, for the very first time in Brooke Bond India Ltd. whereby Raw Coffee Bean Blending as a separate operation, done prior to Roasting, was completely done away with and the Beans Blending process integrated into the Coffee Beans Roasting Process, thereby completely eliminating the need for floor space for the large Raw Coffee Bean Blending Machine and the need for additional man-power required for this operation, both at Coimbatore and at Ghatkesar factories.

65. Modified, renovated and put into operation two new, but inoperable Coffee Roasters made at the Secunderabad Machine Building factory of Brooke Bond, thereby making redundant two very old and obsolete imported Whitmee Coffee Roasters and two very old and obsolete imported Sirrocco Coffee Roasters.

66. Indirectly instrumental in increasing the speed of a large number of Automatic Tea Packing Machines and Tea Hand Packing Benches working in all the other factories in India, in the range of 25 % to 33 %, by setting pioneering examples in Coimbatore factory, during my tenure at Coimbatore, engaging the same existing number of workers per machine.

67. Introduced the concept of Electronic Check Weighing and data collection of individual original Tea Chests on arrival by Load Cell based Electronic Weighing Machines, for the first time in Brooke Bond India Ltd.

68. Demolished a large number of redundant Walls, Partitions, Roofs and Enclosures in the factory, thereby making the Layout of the complete factory more open and spacious, improving ventilation, lighting, cleanliness and facilitating men and material movement. The resultant rubble was used to fill two dry Wells (one of about 10 feet in diameter and about 80 feet deep and another Well of about 40 feet square and about 80 feet deep, together amounting to about 1,25,000 Cubic Foot (equivalent to about 200 Lorry Loads), that were lying empty, dry, unused and open for over 30 years.

69. Removed all Septic Tanks and connected the latrines with the Municipal Sewerage facilities, thereby improved cleanliness and hygiene and eliminate the need for periodic manual cleaning of the Septic Tanks.

70. Relocated two old Oil Storage Tanks and added two new Oil Storage Tanks and constructed a new large Gravure Inks and Solvent Storage Godown, in a new and convenient licensed location to form a Fire and Explosion proof Storage Godown to safely store in bulk the inflammable Gravure Inks and Gravure Solvents, in a manner satisfying the Explosives Act of the government.

71. Modified the old arrangement for Electric Power Mains Distribution with a view to cater to widely varying degrees of government imposed Electric Power Cuts from time to time. Prior to this, some sections of the factory had to be shut down completely when the total power demand of the factory under partial Power Cut exceeded the capacity of the Standby Generator.

72. Replaced all five old, rickety, shabby and narrow Wooden Entry Gates with new and attractive 16 feet wide attractive Steel Fabricated Gates, for better traffic movement and a better aesthetic frontage appearance of the factory compound wall from the road side.

73. Relocated the old Steel Spiral Staircase and Chest Hoist leading from the ground floor at the center of the Tea Packing factory to the higher Blending Department floor, to a more convenient location with a view to reduce congestion and improve material movement.

74. Relocated the complete Bag & Printing Department to a new location that is more convenient for supervision, offered more floor space and reduced material handling and consequently spoils.

75. Relocated the complete storage of Raw Coffee Beans from the outside BLS Godown to inside the factory, thereby completely eliminating two handling and one transport operation and virtually eliminating spillage loss of Raw Coffee Beans during transit.

76. Relocated storing of Packing Materials, which were scattered in different Godowns outside the factory, to inside the factory, in order to facilitate Packing Materials being made available to the respective Departments more quickly, as and when required, thereby also helping to reduce spoils caused as a result of any bad handling.

77. Relocated two Hesser Packing Machines, one Jobday Packing Machine, two Tea Bag Packing Machines, one Cellophane Overwrapping Machine and the Tea Processing Machine inside the Tea factory for better layout and reduced material handling.

78. Relocated the Scrap Yard to a more convenient location.

79. Relocated all the Paste Making Machines to a more convenient location.

80. Relocated all sections of Engineering Department, namely, Electricians Shop, Carpentry, Tin Smithy, Black Smithy and Machine Shop, each of which were situated in separate locations in the factory to a new, convenient and central location, to facilitate better supervision.

81. Relocated the Disintegrator and Chicory storage site inside the factory, thereby eliminating the need for two men permanently engaged in this operation for moving the ground Chicory Powder to the Coffee/Chicory Powder Mixing machine and simultaneously reducing spillage losses of Chicory Powder.

82. Introduced the concept of continuous Pneumatic Evacuation and Conveying of Chicory Powder from the Disintegrator to an Overhead

Hopper, for the very first time in Brooke Bond India Ltd. thereby replacing the previous intermittent and manual removal of the ground Chicory Powder, in batches, from the Receiving Bin installed below the Disintegrator, thereby contributing to increase in productivity, reduction in manual work and offering a much cleaner environment.

83. Introduced the concept of a central Electric Motor driven automatic Diesel Oil Pressure Feed System for the Generator and the two Coffee Roasters by fully automatic feeding of Fuel Oil direct from the underground Storage Tanks, located far away in a safe place, demarcated for storage of combustible fuel in a government approved fire-proof location, which apart from reducing manpower required for daily transfer of Fuel Oil from the Storage Tanks to the various Coffee Roasters and the Electric Power Generator and making the availability of Diesel Oil much more convenient, hassle-free and also virtually eliminating the manual work and resultant spillage of Diesel Oil at different places.

84. I was mainly instrumental in getting both the Congress and CPI led Factory Trade Unions in Coimbatore to accept a Voluntary Retirement Scheme for 75 workers and in return accept a clear Productivity gains of minimum 25 % and up to 33 % with the vast majority of existing Incentive based Production Norms and agreeing to increase the total daily Incentive Wages by Rs. 1.25 only per head and in return, recruit 75 members of their respective families as permanent workers, without affecting the total labour strength of Coimbatore factory and at the same time reducing the total labour cost to the company by a significant margin.

85. Introduced Sprinkler facilities for sprinkling Water throughout the large garden area, thereby reducing requirement of manpower for periodic manual water sprinkling of the large garden and also eliminating water logging in the factory garden.

86. Introduced Pneumatic Dilute Phase Air Conveying of Roasted Coffee Beans from two different Coffee Roasters, through Remote Motor Controlled Rotary Distributors (designed by me and manufactured at Coimbatore factory) to the overhead Buffer Storage Bins of the four different Grinding Machines below.

87. There was a time while I was in Coimbatore that the production requirements of Coffee/Chicory powder mixed products far exceeded the maximum possible output capabilities of the existing two Coffee/

Chicory powder Mixing Machines, even in two shifts. It so happened that there was one new large Duplex Coffee/Chicory powder Mixing Machine, manufactured in Coimbatore under the guidance of I Balasundaram, when he worked as an engineer there, that was lying idle and unused. Balu gave instructions that this machine be installed and commissioned. One problem in this regard was that this was a totally untested and unproven machine, for which no operating standards were available and the only known and acceptable means to implement a working standard was to go entirely by the judgment of a senior Coffee Tasting expert, like C K Ramnath, head of Coffee Tasting and Buying in Brooke Bond. Since I considered this a subjective method, I wanted a more scientific method to go by to decide on this parameter. I discussed this problem with Srinivasan, Head of the Coimbatore branch of the Indian Statistical Institute for a solution and accordingly he recommended a procedure, which I got done as a MBA Thesis Project of a student of PSG College, which established that 25 minutes of mixing time was adequate to give a reasonably uniform and heterogeneous mixture of the Coffee/Chicory Powder Mixture. I was most surprised to learn that the expert Coffee Tasters' opinions matched the results of statistical calculations very accurately.

88. Invented and introduced my simple and patentable Horizontal Radial Continuous Wet Scrubber to trap and collect Chaff released by the Coffee Roasters through its Chimney into the atmosphere, thereby completely eliminating the need for weekly manual cleaning of the Factory Roofs, where the Chaff released through the Roaster Chimneys would accumulate and occasionally choke the Storm Water Roof Drain Pipes.

89. Introduced in 1977, for the first time in Brooke Bond India Ltd., factories a Daro-Soemtron (East German make) computer and got formally approved for use for the very first time in India, an integrated Company Invoice cum Central Excise Gate Pass cum Lorry Loading Slip, fully generated by the computer.

90. Improved the standard of performance and reliability of all the five old company owned cars in the factory, by a very big margin. Prior to this, breakdown of cars, resulting in cars getting stranded outside the factory was really a shockingly frequent occurrence.

91. Re-organised the Main Office to accommodate Factory Manager's office, Reception / Visitor's Room, Tea Sale Room, Central Excise

Office, Bank Counter, Executive's Dining Hall and the Daro-Soemtron Computer office room in a more orderly manner.

92. Introduced new offices for Assistant Factory Manager, Production Manager, Dispatch and Originals Sections in a more convenient and central location inside the factory.

93. Enlarged the Staff Canteen, added Wash Room, Urinal, Store Room and an improved Kitchen.

94. Introduced the JAYEMS Miracle Mill for the grinding of different Spices for Brooke Bond India Ltd.'s Spices division operated by a Contractor in Cochin, for the very first time in Brooke Bond India Ltd.

95. Introduced a novel solution to overcome the problems experienced in roasting small Grain Barley in the Bharat Roasters for Brooke Bond India Ltd.'s Spices division operated by a Contractor in Virudhunagar.

96. Introduced a novel procedure designed specifically to help overcome bias of managers in merit rating of different Staff / Supervisors / Clerks in Coimbatore factory by different managers. This procedure was recognised and accepted as very fair by all the managers of the factory.

97. Relocated the large "BROOKE BOND" Neon Signs from the site of the Administrative Officer's Quarters to a site that is far more prominent and more visible at long distances along the road.

98. A very interesting episode in my life in 1977 (the year of celebrating the centenary of the discovery of recorded sound), while I was at Coimbatore was my invention of an Octagonal Omni-directional Loudspeaker, which when put to a direct A/B comparison test against a Bose Model 901 Series III Loudspeaker (the then flagship speaker of the world famous Bose Corporation, USA), could easily be recognised by any layman as definitely superior to the Bose's loudspeaker at that point in time. It is necessary to point out that I am a mechanical engineer, while loudspeakers come under electrical and electronic engineering. Also, at that point in time, I had not even heard a truly Hi-Fi Loudspeaker, let alone know how to design and make a loudspeaker, or seen the insides of any really good Loudspeaker. My only access to any knowledge regarding Loudspeakers was a small Philips India pocket book size publication titled something like 'Loudspeaker Design Handbook' which cost me about Rs. 15/- in 1977. Since the idea for my Loudspeaker was developed after reading an abridged version of Amar Gopal Bose's PhD thesis on 'Direct/

Reflecting' Loudspeakers and considering that I had no intention, let alone have the necessary expertise, finance and opportunity to go commercial with the manufacture and sale of Loudspeakers, I wrote to Bose himself about my discovery and offered my idea to him for commercial exploitation. In response, I received a letter from Bose's office saying that any new ideas in Loudspeaker technology would be most welcome, but cautioned me about revealing anything about the technology of my Loudspeaker to anyone, until and unless I obtained a Patent for the same in USA. My investigation regarding applying for a Patent in USA revealed that the cost of obtaining such a Patent in USA at that time was totally beyond my reach. This Loudspeaker invented by me, even today, i.e., after over 35 years, can in my personal opinion, rightly qualify for three different claims for Patents. I have with me in my house, an updated version of the same Omni-directional Loudspeaker, made completely with Indian manufactured 'Bolton' Loudspeaker Woofer, Mid-range and Tweeter Drivers.

A photograph of my first Omni-Directional
Loudspeaker made in 1979 can be seen above.

99. I have since made 7 other truly original different designs of Loudspeakers for my friends, including one for Late C S Samuel, ex-Chairman and

Managing Director of Brooke Bond India Ltd. The others for whom I have designed and custom-made new and original design Loudspeakers are,

Shashi Mohanty, V Balaraman, Ashok Kurian, Basant Almal, Basant Almal's Lawyer, Samiran Das, Kumar Srinivasan, Das and Sen.

100. I followed up this work on Loudspeakers with the creation of a Belt Driven, Record Player the ON/OFF Switch and the Speed Control Switch of which was operated with touch control and fitted with a Stroboscope to vary and visually control the correct speed of rotation of the Platter (33, or 45 RPM), an imported SME Pickup Arm and a SHURE V 15 Type III Cartridge, both acknowledged to be one of the world's best, at that point in time, which can be seen in the picture below:

While at BROOKE HOUSE, KOLKATA, 1979 – 1987.

101. Visited a total of 35 different factories of Packaging Machine and Gravure Printing Machine manufacturers in UK, Germany, France, Spain, Italy and Switzerland, in one single solo trip, spread over 35 days, in 1983. This was done primarily with a view to explore the scope and feasibility of introducing a totally new Packaging System to replace the existing Wood's Pice Packet Packing System that had matured to its maximum practical operating speed from 60 to 220 Packets per minute, i.e., by 265 %, using the same man power and while being the cheapest operating mechanized Automatic Packaging System for any Product, in any size, using any Packing Material, in any country, anywhere in the world. The trip was an outstanding success, resulting in my framing of and proving the workability of a totally new and much more modern Packaging System that is cheaper and superior to the existing Packaging System and viable even today. It is another extremely sad story that this unique and valuable concept or project, that is the biggest and best project in my working career, was killed without seeing the light of the day, by the mishandling of the complete project by my superiors. The list of factories visited by me in Europe for this purpose can be seen in **Annexure B** towards the end of this note**.**

102. Following my visit to Europe, I Invented and introduced a totally new, original and possibly patentable concept of a Hot Melt Adhesive Pattern Coated Sachet Packing Machine with a view to produce Pice Packets, offering a cheaper and at the same time more attractive and modern looking Pice Packets. This was to replace the more than 80 year old Wood's Pice Packet Machine and the more modern Berkshire Gravure Printing cum Bag Making Machine, which when combined together, offered the cheapest Pouch Packing System for any product, of any size, in any form of Packet, Sachet, or Pouch in the whole world, from its very inception in the 1930s till today, i.e., till 2016. Auke Van de Clerk, Chief Engineer, Unilever PLC, UK openly commented at a meeting in Bangalore that "*for this one Project Report alone, Chandy, you truly deserve a PhD*".

103. Designed and got made a totally new 300 Kg Batch Size Jabez Burn cum Probat type hybrid Coffee Roasting Machine in 1988, for the first time in Brooke Bond India Ltd. with a view to combine the best

features of the American Jabez Burn and the German Probat Roasters in one totally new hybrid Coffee Roaster that can be seen below.

This is perhaps, till today, the largest Automatic Batch type Coffee Roaster ever manufactured by anybody in India, including PROBAT Werke von Gimborn Maschinenfabrik GmbH, the global market leader in manufacturing Roasting machines and plants who also manufacture Roasting machines in India.

104. Introduced Kilburn & Co., a division of McNeill & Magor, Mumbai, which had a technical collaboration with Stork Bowen, USA, as a totally new supplier for the new Instant Coffee Plant coming up at Hosur, thereby not only helping to introduce an alternate source to the only other reputable and existing source in India, namely, Larsen & Toubro, Mumbai, who had a technical collaboration with Niro, Denmark, who till then had a virtual monopoly hold on the Indian market. This introduction also helped introduce competition and thereby reduce the capital cost for the new Instant Coffee Plant coming up in Hosur by a very significant margin.

105. Conceived and developed a full set of manufacturing drawings to make a fully automatic Match Skillet 4-colour Gravure Printing and Strike Compound Coating Machine, equipped with Radio Frequency Driers to be imported from Strayfield Wiles International, UK, to dry the Water Based Strike Compound applied on the two sides of the Cardboard Match Skillets, to meet the requirement of Hind Matches

Ltd. a major Match maker in Sivakasi, Tamil Nadu. The project had to be abandoned after completing the full set of manufacturing drawings and working out the sale price and the customer ready to place the Purchase Order, on account of an unexpectedly large increase in Central Excise Duty on Matches by the government, making the project unviable for the intended customer.

106. Designed a reduced scale Tower Blender of 4-Tons batch size for the very first time in Brooke Bond India Ltd. in India (compared to the standard 6-Ton batch sizes of all other Tower Blenders operating in Brooke Bond India Ltd.) specifically for Brooke Bond India Ltd.'s export requirements met by a Contract Packer, namely, Kishore International, Agra.

107. Negotiated and sold a set of six identical four-colour 20-inches wide Gravure Printing cum Rewinding Machines, through one single purchase order, from HGF Laminates Pvt. Ltd., belonging to the Paharpur Cooling Towers Group. This is the largest single Purchase Order ever received by Brooke Bond for sale of any Printing or Packaging Machines.

108. Designed and got manufactured by Vendors in Kolkata, three different models of coin operated Condom Vending Machines for dispensing Nirodh Condoms, as Brooke Bond India Ltd.'s contribution to the Indian government for their Family Planning Drive, all over India.

109. Developed a remarkably simple, quick and reliable method to scale up, or scale down by any reasonable ratio, a fully scaled CAD drawing of any Key-line drawing of the Art Work of any Packet Label, or Fascia of any Packet, Carton, etc., by just one stroke on the Keyboard of a computer.

While at BROOKEFIELDS, BANGALORE, 1987 to 1995.

110. Got made by a Vendor and sold one 225 Kgs batch size Jabez Burns type Coffee Bean Roaster to Kannan Jubilee Coffee Co., Coimbatore.

111. Introduced successfully a novel and simple concept of reducing shrinkage in the weight of Coffee Beans during roasting, for the first time at Whitefield factory in Brooke Bond India Ltd. and possibly in India and abroad.

After RETIREMENT in September 1995, till today.

112. Took up a Consultancy assignment for Hindustan Lever Ltd. to create, conceptualize and set up an integrated Plant for Cleaning, Blending, Moisture Reducing and Bulk Vacuum Packing of Teas meant primarily for export of Teas to Japan, at the factory of Lipton India Exports Ltd. Kidderpore, Kolkata. The Cleaning part of this process was my discovery / invention, introduced for the very first time in India and possibly elsewhere. According to information available with me, the process developed by me is a far superior process compared to the equivalent Cleaning processes employed by several specialist Cleaning companies in operation in Japan. I am now working on applying for a Patent for an improved process for the same.

113. Arranged the purchase and sale of five used and condemned as obsolete and scrapped, Brooke Bond India Ltd. made Berkshire Printing cum Paper Bag Making Machines to M/s D J Malpani, Sangamner, Maharashtra, India's largest Chewing Tobacco Dealer. I also helped Malpani in setting up and reconditioning all these five Machines to such a high level of quality standards that the quality and performance levels of all these five old and scrapped machines far exceeded the quality and performance levels of any similar old, or new machines that ever worked anywhere and at any time in Brooke Bond India Ltd. in the past.

114. Invented and got manufactured by Rollatainers Ltd. at their Machine Building Factory in Peenya, Bangalore, on a Royalty basis, 34 totally new and original design fully automatic Paper Bag Pouch Packing Machines capable of producing a triple fold and labeled Pouch, at 200+ Packets per minute. A picture of the same machine can be seen below. This helped completely convert the previous working method of India's leading Chewing Tobacco Dealer, M/s D J Malpani, Sangamner, Maharashtra from complete manual packing of about 25,00,000 Chewing Tobacco Packets per day, to packing about 50,00,000 Chewing Tobacco Packets per day, automatically and entirely by the 34 machines, thereby helping to reduce their previous level of man-power requirement by about 600 persons by way of a Voluntary Retirement Scheme and at the same time not only helping to reduce cost of Packing but also simultaneously improve quality

and aesthetic finish of the Packets. Taking into account the increase in production from the previous levels of about 25,00,000 Chewing Tobacco Packets per day, fully with manual labour, to currently packing about 50,00,000 Chewing Tobacco Packets per day, fully by machines, would imply that the gross equivalent reduction in the total man-power requirement to realise this higher level of output, over the initial output would be well over 1,200 men.

115. Invented, designed, got manufactured 173 totally new Bulk Density Meters, of which 119 Nos. conform to a new standard set by me and 54 Nos. fully conform to Internationally recognised and accepted ISO standards. I continue to get Royalty on each and every Bulk Density Meter manufactured and sold in the market by a party in Bangalore. Of these Bulk Density Meters, 48 Bulk Density Meters are currently in use by Factories, Sale Rooms, Packaging Development Units and at Quality Control offices of Hindustan Unilever throughout India, 50 Bulk Density Meters by Tata Global Beverages Ltd., 10 by Duncans Tea Ltd., and lesser

numbers by a large number of companies dealing in Tea and other products.

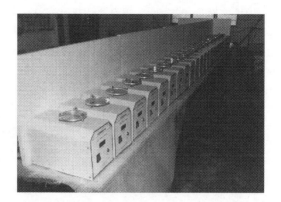

116. Set up a 13.4 Cubic Meter (6,000 Kgs) batch size Tower type Tea Blending Plant for Akbar Brothers Ltd. Colombo, Sri Lanka, which is by far the largest Tea Blender cum Packer cum Exporter in Sri Lanka. Testimonials from an Owner cum Director of this company can be seen in my website – www.chandyjohn.com.

117. Introduced the concept of below-the-ground In-Feed Hopper for the first time anywhere, for Akbar Brothers Ltd. Sri Lanka, which greatly helped reduce the physical strain to workers by having to lift the heavy Tea filled Plywood Chests, Bags or Sacks from the ground level and tip the contents of Tea over the 1+ meter high Rim of the in-feed Hopper. The below-the-ground Pit is covered totally dust-tight to prevent any ingress of even the smallest quantity of Tea into the Pit and covered by easily removable and interchangeable Metal Covers.

This is a cheaper substitute for the imported expensive Vacuum Assisted Pick and Place Unit made in UK or Germany. Two other versions of an equivalent below-the-ground In-feed Hoppers set up in Colombo and in Jeddah, Saudi Arabia and can be seen below.

118. Set up a 4,000 Kgs per Hour Tea Cleaning Plant integrated with a 10 Cubic Meter (4,500 Kgs) batch size Tower type Tea Blending Plant, the first of its kind in the world, for MJF Teas Pvt. Ltd. (owners of the internationally famous and highly reputed DILMAH Brand of Teas), Colombo, Sri Lanka. MJF Teas now clean and blend their entire requirement of their Teas on this Plant. Testimonials from Malik J Fernando, part Owner cum Director of this company can be seen in the Testimonial Section of my website – www.chandyjohn.com.

119. Set up a 4.2 Cubic Meter (1,000 Kgs) batch size fully automatic Drum type Tea Blending Plant with below-the-ground-In-Feed Hopper, for A M S Baeshen & Co., Jeddah, Saudi Arabia, that bettered the output performance of a virtually identical fully automatic Drum type Tea Blending Plant supplied by Mr. Gordon J Barnes, UK, (a world leading and highly reputed designer cum manufacturer cum supplier of Tea Blending Machines), about 8 years earlier, to Baeshen & Co., by a surprising margin of over 98 % and sold at an unbelievably low price of UK £ 77,101/- compared to the last negotiated price of about UK £ 275,000/-) quoted by the same UK supplier. Baeshen, owners of the RABEA Brand of Teas, is the leader in Tea trade in Saudi Arabia, holding about 80 % market share of the Packet Tea trade in Saudi Arabia, as on 2000. This Blending Plant has been working very satisfactorily till today and is expected to give equally good performance for several decades into the future. A M S Baeshen & Co., were so immensely impressed and satisfied with the improvements in the Tea Blending Plant proposed to be supplied and promised by me to achieve a performance superior to that of their existing Gordon Barnes'

UK made Plant, that they placed a Purchase Order, at the outset and without even seeing any of my other Plants either in operation, or even in idle condition anywhere, for all necessary accessories and equipment that were additionally required to increase the output performance of the original Tea Blending Plant supplied by Barnes by an equal margin of over 98 %. Testimonials from the senior management Team of this company and the report on the measured outputs of the two Plants can be seen in my website – www.chandyjohn.com.

120. Set up a 7,000 Kgs per Hour Tea Cleaning Plant integrated with a 8.4 Cubic Meter (2.75 Ton) batch size (21 Cu. Mtrs. total internal volume) Drum type Tea Blending Plant, the first of its kind in the world, for Van Rees Ceylon Ltd., Colombo, Sri Lanka, which is the largest division of the multinational company, Van Rees B V., The Netherlands, the world's leading independent Tea Dealer/Supplier. Testimonials from the different senior management team members of this company can be seen in my website – www.chandyjohn.com.

121. The Blending Drum of the Van Rees' Tea Blending Plant, to the best of my knowledge, is the largest Blending Drum (21 Cubic Meters total internal volume) used for blending Tea anywhere, at least till 2006, when it was set up. Testimonials to this effect from the senior management Team of the Dutch owned Van Rees Ceylon Ltd. a division of Van Rees B V, Rotterdam, can be seen in my website – www.chandyjohn.com.

122. This Van Rees Tea Blending Plant is, to the best of my knowledge, the first large scale Tea Blending Plant in the world that can handle the exceptionally long leaf Ceylon Orthodox type OPA, OP and OP1 Grade Teas (with an average Bulk Density of 5.7 Liters per Kg). Certificates to this effect from the senior management Team of Van Rees can be seen in my website – www.chandyjohn.com.

123. This Van Rees Tea Blending Plant is, to the best of my knowledge, the first Tea Blending Machine in the world that can not only match, but exceed the quality and performance levels of manual blending of the same Teas on the Floor, in respect of uniformity of mix, breakage of Tea Particles and loss of Bloom. Until then, it was generally believed widely in the Tea trade, the world over, that no Tea Blending Machine can equal, or let alone exceed the quality and performance levels of a properly executed manual blending process, of the same Teas, on

the Floor. Certificates to this effect from the senior management Team of Van Rees Ceylon Ltd. can be seen in my website – www.chandyjohn.com.

Plans for the future.

124. Invented a novel and patentable Process / Plan to form granulate Tea Particles of any size, for the first time in the world, as confirmed by a formal World-wide Patent Search, carried out by my Patent Attorney. Tea Particles only progressively reduce in size as it passes through various stages in the manufacturing, blending and packing process, resulting in loss of its market value, esteem and price. Employing the Process invented by me, it is now feasible to convert a low market demand, low value, small size Particle Teas into a higher market demand, higher value, larger size Particle Teas, without the addition of any water, or any kind of binder. A second advantage gained by this process is that the unpleasant phenomenon of very small particles of Teas percolating through the porous Tea Bag Filter Paper and settling down at the bottom, on the inside of the Tea Bag Cartons and also on the outside between the transparent Plastic Overwrap Film and the Carton, thereby presenting an ungainly and ugly visual appearance. This can be completely eliminated by first sifting, separating and removing all the small size Tea Particles, then Granulating and enlarging the Particle size as required and then putting it back into the bulk Tea, before it is packed into Tea Bags. This invention as developed by me till now has the potential for application in all Tea Estates, Tea Blending and Tea Packing factories not only in India, but throughout the world and has the scope for further improvement.

125. While my Tea Cleaning Process is working very satisfactorily with all grades of Orthodox Teas at four different locations, I am now working on applying for a Patent for an improved Tea Cleaning Process invented by me and to be developed to work especially with CTC Teas with its high content of Fine Dust Teas, which would normally be carried away with other impurities like, Dust, Tea Fluff, etc., and have to be disposed of as waste and therefore not acceptable to the Tea industry in general.

126. Conceived a Process / Plan to adopt an existing Classifying Machine to separate Stalk from Teas, as an alternate method to employing the widely used / traditional / conventional / expensive / low output Camera-based Optical Colour Sorting Machines. The Classifying Machines identified by me, offer very much higher throughputs compared to the Optical / Camera-based Colour Sorting Machines and at the same time cost very much less per Kg of Output per Hour. This Classifying Machine is also much more versatile than the commonly used Camera-based Optical Colour Sorting Machine, thereby presenting scope to grade the Teas into a variety of Grades other than pure Stalk, which is the only possibility with the Camera-based Optical Colour Sorting Machines. The Camera-based Optical Colour Sorting Machines are much more complex in design compared to the Classifying Machines identified by me, which on the other hand are very simple, easy to understand and operate by average skilled technicians. The Camera-based Optical Colour Sorting Machines requires specialized knowledge of Optics and Electronics and experience to be able to handle and operate these Machines. This concept has the potential for application in all Tea Estates not only in India, but throughout the world. While I am quite optimistic that the idea will work, the process has yet to be tried out, waiting for the right Tea company to work with me in this endeavor.

127. Conceived a Process / Plan to automatically pick up and transfer Withered Tea Leaves from the Withering Troughs direct to the CTC, or Rolling Machines, through Pneumatic Conveying Tubes, thereby reducing man-power requirement significantly and at the same time eliminate spillage and cross-contamination with other impurities during its handling and transit. This concept has the potential for application in all Tea Estates not only in India, but throughout the world. While I am quite optimistic that the idea will work, the process has yet to be tried out, waiting for the right Tea company to work with me in this endeavor.

128. Conceived a Process / Plan whereby Green Tea after the Process of Withering, Rolling / Cutting, Fermenting is partially dried in a conventional Endless Chain Pressure (ECP) or Fluid Bed Drier (FBD) and then passed through a Microwave Drier to bring down the Moisture Level from its existing level to the final desired 1.5 % to 2.0 %

level, subjecting the fermented Teas to lower temperatures than those encountered in ECP or FBD Driers. This Process, if implemented in a way proposed by me, will result in the reduction of total Energy Cost and simultaneously improve the quality and hence increase the market value of the Tea. This Process / Plan has the potential for application in all Tea Estates not only in India, but throughout the world. While I am quite optimistic that the idea will work, the process has yet to be tried out, waiting for the right Tea company to work with me in this endeavor.

129. Conceived a Plan to add a small dose worth about Rs. 0.50 of a synthetic Liquid Flavour to a Kg. of Darjeeling Tea, whereby the estimated market value of the Tea gets enhanced by about Rs. 15.00 a Kg., as estimated by the Sale Room Director – Tea, Brooke Bond India Ltd. This result was developed in the first attempt and results of much higher value can be had if more work is put into developing the process. As such a Flavour enhanced Tea cannot be legally and commercially sold, for sale within India, I am waiting for a Tea exporter interested to take up and work on this venture, in co-operation with me.

130. Conceived a Process / Plan to make a fully automatic High Speed Beedi Making Machine using Cigarette Paper as an alternate Outer Wrapper, instead of the traditional Tendu Leaves, used for making a very economical Beedis. This Process/Plan has the potential for application in all major Beedi making and selling companies in India to reduce manpower requirement drastically, increase output, improve quality and reduce cost.

131. As the White Cigarette Paper will not easily find acceptance by traditional Beedi users, due to the absence of the traditional Tendu Leaves, a plan was conceived by me to print the Cigarette Paper with the Tendu Leaf design and then emboss the Paper with the design, style and shape of the Veins of a typical Tendu Leaf, in order to create a Paper Beedi that visually looks almost like the traditional Tendu Leaf made Beedi. This Process/Plan has the potential for application in all major Beedi making and selling companies in India. While I am quite optimistic that the idea will work, the process has yet to be tried out, waiting for the right Beedi company to work in partnership with me in this endeavor.

132. Conceived a Process/Plan to make a fully automatic Beedi Making Machine employing a Camera based Robotic arrangement to work with Tendu Leaves and make a traditional Beedi, fully and automatically by machine. This Process/Plan has the potential for application in all major Beedi making and selling companies in India. While I am quite optimistic that the idea will work, the process has yet to be tried out, waiting for the right Beedi company to work with in partnership with me in this endeavor.

133. Conceived and working on an integrated Process / Plan to automatically slit, open, dump, bulk, clean and then load onto ships, Sacks containing 55 KG Wheat packed in separate PP Woven Sacks delivered in 175 to 200 Railway Wagons per day for export in ships, by the Adani Group at the Mundra Port in Gujarat.

ANNEXURE B

List of the Factories of Companies in Europe visited by me in one trip over a span of 35 days in 1983, in connection with my exploratory work related to the Pice Packet Project.

1. Brooke Bond Liebig Ltd., UK.
2. Rose Forgrove Ltd., UK.
3. Strayfield Wiles International, UK.
4. Europack Engineering Co. Ltd., UK.
5. The General Engineering Co., (Radcliffe) Ltd., UK.
6. ArcelorMittal Mouzon, France.
7. Siebler Verpackungstechnik GmbH + Co. KG, W. Germany.
8. Fawema GmbH, W. Germany.
9. Rowema Verpackungsmaschinen GmbH, W. Germany.
10. Robert Bosch GmbH, W. Germany.
11. Hassia Verpackungsmaschinen GmbH, W. Germany.
12. Teepack Spezialmaschinen GmbH & Co., W. Germany.
13. Maschinenfabrik Max Kroenert GmbH + Co., W. Germany.
14. Fischer & Krecke GmbH (Bobst Group), W. Germany.
15. Schober GmbH, W. Germany.
16. Bobst S. A., Switzerland.
17. SIG Swiss Industrial Co., Switzerland.
18. RMH-Maschinenbau AG, Switzerland.
19. Polytype SA, Switzerland.
20. MDC Max Dätwyler AG, Switzerland.
21. Cerutti Giovanni Officine Meccaniche S.p.A., Italy.
22. Schiavi S.p.A., Italy.
23. Andreotti, Italy.
24. Rotomec S. p. A., Italy.
25. IMA Industries S.r.l., Italy.
26. Universal Pack, Italy.
27. Goglio Luigi. Milano. S. P. A., Italy.
28. Segafredo, Italy
29. ICA S. p. A., Italy.
30. Dott. Bonapace & C., Italy.
31. Scholari Engineering S. R. L., Italy.

32. Mapimpianti spa. Italy.
33. Volpack S. A., Spain.
34. Construcciones Mecanicas Guill, Spain.
35. Rotatek, Spain.

For any further information, or clarifications, please write, or send email to my address given below, giving your full name, company name and full mailing address, your position in the company, landline and mobile phone numbers, email ID and the background, and / or purpose for which you are seeking the information, or clarification. Please feel free to write and ask for obligation-free information, or clarification, even if your end purpose is for any commercial applications.

Except where Patents are involved, any information given above can be used by anyone without giving any credit to me, as long as you do not try to take credit for the same.

Chandy John
D-304 Athashri Whitefield
6th Cross, Prithvi Layout
Whitefield,
Bangalore, INDIA – 560066
Phone: +91-(0)9845006126
Email: chandyjohn@gmail.com
Website: www.chandyjohn.com
Skype ID: chandyj
Sep. 1, 2016

My Brother-in-law, my wife, Leela and myself with Pundit Jawaharlal Nehru

Leela and myself with Sunil Gavaskar

Leela with Sherpa Tenzing Norgay

Leela with Mother Teresa

Printed in the United States
By Bookmasters